U0962389

体裁互文性研究

A Study in Generic Intertextuality

陈亚萍 著

中央高校基本科研业务费专项资金资助
Supported by the Fundamental Research Funds for the Central Universities

同濟大學出版社
TONGJI UNIVERSITY PRESS

内 容 提 要

本书为体裁互文研究建构了一个突破语篇层面的宏观的三维理论框架模型，在符号学范畴中将一个宏观社会符号观引入了体裁互文性的研究中。

全书共八章。第一章介绍研究的起源、理论、目的和本书的组织框架；第二章文献综述，整理了涉及体裁互文性的已有相关研究成果，并进行评述；第三章在重新界定体裁互文性的基础上，论证了在符号学范畴下建立宏观社会符号理论体系的必要性，并推导出体裁互文研究三维理论模型；第四章到第六章分别对该三维理论模型中的三个维度，即体裁互文系统，体裁互文过程，体裁互文焦点做了深入探讨；第七章是尝试该理论模型指导英语教学实践；第八章总结了本书的主要结论，并指出了对体裁互文性进行深入研究的方向。

本书可供语言学专业的教师、学生及其他从事语言学研究的相关人员阅读使用。

图书在版编目(CIP)数据

体裁互文性研究 / 陈亚萍著. --上海：同济大学出版社，2019.10

ISBN 978-7-5608-8480-6

Ⅰ.①体… Ⅱ.①陈… Ⅲ.①社会语言学—研究 Ⅳ.①H0

中国版本图书馆 CIP 数据核字(2019)第 198265 号

体裁互文性研究

陈亚萍 **著**

责任编辑 张智中 **责任校对** 徐春莲 **封面设计** 钱如潺

出版发行 同济大学出版社 www.tongjipress.com.cn
(地址：上海市四平路 1239 号 邮编：200092 电话：021-65985622)

经　　销 全国各地新华书店
排　　版 南京月叶图文制作有限公司
印　　刷 大丰科星印刷有限责任公司
开　　本 787 mm×1092 mm 1/16
印　　张 10.75
字　　数 268 000
版　　次 2019 年 10 月第 1 版 2019 年 10 月第 1 次印刷
书　　号 ISBN 978-7-5608-8480-6

定　　价 39.00 元

前　言

体裁互文性作为一个热门课题，在批评性研究领域中是指"不同语篇体裁或类型之间的现今的或历史的关系，每一种语篇体裁或类型都是以一个集合主体或一类使用者为前提的，因为每一类语篇都是受到某个社会团体、阶层或机构的控制，不同的社会组织对不同的语篇体裁或类型具有优先权"。在体裁研究领域，体裁互文性则被定义为体裁的动态性和混合性，因为体裁是动态的和历史性的，它总会对社会体系其他方面的动态变化做出反应。

对体裁互文性的不同定义指向以下共识性问题。第一，体裁互文性是有关体裁的语言交际现象，不可避免地将以体裁研究为基础。因而，对体裁本质属性的理解是完善体裁互文性研究的基础。第二，体裁互文和社会意识形态之间存在着密切的联系，具有宏观社会符号意义。对这一宏观社会符号的内涵进行探讨是必要的。第三，体裁互文既涉及社会性的、历史性的异质体裁混合系统，又最终体现为一种动态的反应过程。体裁互文性研究既应涵盖对体裁互文的形式描述，又应有对体裁互文的认知性发生机制的探讨，理应是一个多维度、多层级的研究。鉴于此，本书认为有必要建立一个多维度的宏观层面的体裁互文性研究理论框架。

本书为体裁互文性研究所建立的理论框架是一个宏观社会符号理论框架。符号学和语言学的结合是由来已久的努力方向，其结合的可行性、有效性以及使得语言研究更全面的价值早有定论。本书通过分析索绪尔、皮尔斯，以及之后的韩礼德等人对语言符号的观点，提出了一个关于语言及其周围环境的宏观社会符号体系。这一体系的构建明确了语篇、语域、体裁以及意识形态之间的关系。本书论证了将语篇视作为一个完整象征符号而非语言符号复合体的合理性和必要性，并在此基础上提出，体裁作为语言符号宏观体系中的最高层面，其实质是宏观社会符号过程体系(macro social semiosis system)。于是，体裁互文性可被定义为宏观社会符号过程体系中各成分元素之间的互动关系。这一关系本身又可视作为一种符号过程。借鉴对语言符号两分法的研究方法，本书分别对体裁互文系统和体裁互文过程进行研究，并基于对语言及其周围环境的宏观社会符号体系的建构和分析，进一步发展了体裁互文性研究理论框架的第三个维度，体裁互文焦点。至此，一个三维体裁互文性研究理论框架模型被建构起来，包括体裁互文系统、体裁互文过程及体裁互文焦点三个维度。

在体裁互文系统的维度上，体裁互文被视作一个含有若干体裁互文潜势的资源系统，具体包括体裁互文学科知识潜势(disciplinary knowledge potentials)，体裁互文宏观话语行为潜势(macro-speech act potentials)，体裁互文评价潜势(evaluation potentials)，以及体裁互文模态潜势(modality potentials)。本书对于体裁互文系统中各个潜势的论断是在体裁研究，以及符号多模态研究的基础之上的。体裁本质属性和体裁定性标准为体裁互文系统中的学科知识潜势、体裁互文宏观话语行为潜势、体裁互文评价潜势提供了有力的理论依据，而符号学对多模态的研究则为体裁互文模态潜势的提出提供了必要的理论支持。

如果说本书对体裁互文系统的讨论是探究体裁互文活动中有哪些资源可供选择参与，那么对体裁互文过程的探讨则是试图回答体裁互文是如何得以实现，或者说是尝试性地对体裁互文发生过程的认知机制作出解释。对体裁互文的认知机制的探讨包括两个方面：首先是对体裁互文系统中各个潜势的认知模型进行讨论；然后在此基础上提出，体裁互文过程可以被理解为一种概念整合过程，因此完全可以借用空间整合理论来解释体裁互文过程的概念整合机制。根据心理空间整合理论，概念整合过程涉及四个心理空间，两个输入空间，一个类属空间和一个整合空间。由体裁互文资源系统中的不同潜势元素组成的输入空间，经过类属空间操作机制处理后，被整合成一个以体裁互文潜势元素混合为特质的动态解释空间。这一过程就是具有概念整合性质的体裁互文过程。

本书的研究始终坚持语言符号观，将体裁视为宏观社会符号过程体系，体裁互文涉及的是宏观社会符号过程体系中各成分元素之间的关系，所以强调符号"解释项"的存在价值。体裁互文中所涉及的解释是一种选择性的解释，因而不得不考虑体裁互文过程中选择的动机(motivation)，也就是体裁互文研究的第三个维度——体裁互文焦点。体裁互文焦点的讨论旨在借用行动理论对决定体裁互文参与者为何选择体裁空间中的某种体裁互文潜势元素参与体裁互文，即参与者的选择动机，作出解释。某种意义上，对体裁互文焦点的讨论是对体裁互文过程的补充性探讨。动机所操控的就是体裁输入空间中的体裁互文潜势焦点。本书认为，是"意图"(intention)操控和决定了体裁互文过程中的焦点选择。本书在建构语言及其环境的宏观符号系统时，论证了意识形态与系统的各个层面之间都存在一种监控和影响的互动关系。意识形态对体裁互文的监控和影响作用是通过意图得以实现的。

在建构了体裁互文性研究的三维理论框架后，本书将进一步从理论层面上得出的结论应用于对英语教学领域的实践指导中，以期为英语教学实践提供参考性指导。

总之，本书旨在为体裁互文研究建构一个突破语篇层面的宏观的三维理论框架模型，在符号学范畴中将一个宏观社会符号观引入了体裁互文性的研究中。期望本书不仅能对体裁互文现象的意义、价值，现象背后的认知机制，以及其与社会建构之间的关系有更深刻的认识和理解，同时也期望对英语实践领域及其他研究领域提供实践指导和理论参考。

由于作者水平有限，若书中有不妥之处，恳请广大学者斧正。

著 者

2019 年 8 月

Contents

List of Figures and Table

Chapter One

Introduction

1.1 Origins of the Study

Since Zellig Harris first proposed the notion of discourse analysis in 1952, studies in discourses or texts have received more and more attention in various fields. Greatly influenced by the achievements from other booming disciplines, such as computer science, social linguistics, as well as philosophy of language, discourse or text studies challenge the traditional approach of syntax with discourses, and text is researched beyond clauses or treated as more than a sequence of clauses.

Once discourses or texts are studied beyond clauses, discourses or texts have to be treated as passages in the form of a unified whole. As Halliday and Hasan state, the word TEXT is used in linguistics to refer to any passage, spoken or written, of whatever length, that does form a unified whole. Best regarded as a semantic unit, a text is a unit of language in use rather than a grammatical unit that is like a sentence. (*Cohesion in English* 1—2) This view has been well supported. It is impossible to find essential properties of discourses or texts when considering them as a collection of sentences with individualist ideology and without reference to other factors. Actually, it is by the involvement of context, interaction, and cognition etc. that studies in discourses or texts can be conducted in a way more explanatory than descriptive. Therefore, discourse analysis or text linguistics is turning to the process of production and interpretation of discourses or texts with its central task of studying discourses or texts in the perspective of construction and function. And meanwhile, discourse analysis or text linguistics is extended in a broader sense and established in an interdisciplinary field.

When a discourse or text is explained rather than described and as process rather than product, intertextuality as one of the essential properties and criteria for text is highlighted and being explored a lot. The notion of intertextuality was proposed less than fifty years ago, but has been a hot research issue in various fields. Although it has been defined differently in different fields, it has been widely accepted that intertextuality implies the inevitable interdependence between texts by the reference of texts to other texts or the textual transcendence of the text. In Bakhtin's words,

> the text lives only by coming into contact with another text (with context). Only at this point of contact between texts does a light flash, illuminating both the posterior and anterior, jointing a given text to a dialogue. We emphasize that this contact is a dialogic contact between texts ... (qtd. in Bauman 2)

Intertextuality has been well studied in various domains, such as applied linguistics, systemic functional linguistics, text linguistics and critical discourse analysis. By virtue of their achievements, we may conclude that intertextuality not only emphasizes the importance of prior texts but also stresses the contributions made by prior texts to a code which renders the various effects of signification. Intertextuality should be considered as a designation of its participation in the discursive space of a culture. It implies that the study of intertextuality is not the investigation of sources and influences as traditionally conceived; it casts its net wider to include anonymous discursive practices, codes whose origins are lost, that make possible the signifying practices of later texts. (Culler 103) In this sense, intertextuality is a very complex and multi-dimensional concept. And it seems more significant to explore how intertextuality can be accomplished than to superficially describe relationship among texts.

Generic intertextuality as a type of intertextuality has been chosen as the topic of our dissertation. We choose it because of its significance in today's society. First of all, genre has been proven to be of social meanings. With the linguistic-oriented tendency, genre in terms of linguistics has been focused on as an effective means for manipulating social and institutional activities. The continuous emergence of new genres more requires our attention to the operative mechanism of genre creation, that is, generic intertextuality. At the same time, by studies in generic intertextuality, some transformation of social practices and change of institutional conventions or ideologies can be exhibited.

Generic intertextuality has been discussed a lot and has been defined differently in different perspectives. In critical approach, it "is mainly concerned with current or historical relations between genres or types of discourse, each of which can be seen as presupposing a collective subject or a kind of addressees in the sense that each type of discourse is more or less in the monopoly of a social group, a class or an institution and different social sections are privileged by different discourse types". (Xin Bin, *Intertextuality from a Critical Perspective* 93) In generic studies, generic intertextuality refers to the dynamic and mixture of genres, since genres are dynamic and historical, responding to the dynamics of other parts of social systems. That is to say, although any text must be of genre, it can never belong to only one genre. The generic intertextuality or the heterogeneity of genres is always in any text. And it is further argued that all genres may mix together and no hard border among them. Thus, some relevant notions to show the heterogeneity of genres are proposed, such as genre set, system of genre, genre colony, genre network, etc.

Although generic intertextuality has been studied a lot, the delimitation of generic intertextuality is still far from definite and the studies in it are not satisfactory. There are several limitations. First of all, generic intertextuality is a type of intertextuality mainly involving genres. But since the elements of orders of discourse are extremely diverse and it is by no means easy to decide whether one is dealing with genres, styles, discourses, or whatever, there is not and could not be, a determinate list of genres, styles or discourses, and it often appears to be a rather arbitrary decision about whether something is or is not a separate instance of one of these types. (Fairclough, *Discourse and Social Change* 125) In this sense, the lack of established terminology for genres, styles and discourse types hinders the exploration of generic intertextuality.

Secondly, it seems that the previous studies in generic intertextuality tend to focus on the variations in generic strategies in formal ways. The formal features of generic intertextuality are more discussed, while the issues on how the producers and receivers in particular discourse communities do with other intertextualized discourses when generic intertextuality occurs are less addressed. Most of studies talk about what generic intertextuality looks like or why it is there. Specifically speaking, studies in generic intertextuality are more a kind of descriptive studies not fully or deeply explanatory, although the communicative purposes have been involved in generic approach. The formal features or linguistic resources of generic intertextuality are paid more attention to, while the mechanism of generic intertextuality has been less involved. It is true that studies in generic intertextuality in critical approach have tried to discuss the causes of generic intertextuality and proposed that generic intertextuality is developed from social ideology. However, the studies are only conducted within the domain of critical linguistics or in a critical approach, which decides them impossible to be complete and satisfactory. In short, there is very little attempting to integrate the socio-cognitive factors that so often contribute to the act of genre construction, interpretation, use and exploitation to achieve non-linguistic ends in real life. (Bhatia, *Worlds of Written Discourse* 112) No cognitive mechanism of generic intertextuality concerning how generic intertextuality happens has been involved. But it is probably an area worth further research.

Thirdly, although the mutual-influencing relationship between generic intertextuality and ideologies has been well accepted in studies in generic intertextuality in critical approach, no further details about any operable linkage between them are explored. We have not got full ideas about how to realize the association between generic intertextuality and ideologies, or what the carrier of ideology is and in what way ideologies function in generic intertextuality.

Fourthly, the theoretical basis for generic intertextuality seems not convincing or sensible enough. Studies in generic intertextuality are variously conducted based on different theoretical assumptions. Each rationale for any study to base on is partly convincing and sensible since it only concerns one perspective or dimension of generic intertextuality. In some sense, it is the lack of inclusive and powerful rationale that results in some of limitations mentioned above.

And furthermore, when we talk about the interdiscursivity of a text which is realized in semantic, grammatical and lexical features of the text, we actually explore generic intertextuality at the level of discourse rather than group of discourses or genre. Interdiscursivity concerns only configuration of genre, that is, discourse. After all, every discourse must be of genre. Thus, we may well suggest the necessity of constructing a more macro and powerful or inclusive rationale for studies in generic intertextuality.

1.2 Rationale for the Study

We try to construct a powerful and inclusive rationale, specifically a macro social semiotic framework, which is expected to make up for the deficiencies or limitations in former generic intertextuality studies.

It is well known that semiology is first proposed by the great linguist Saussure. According to Saussure, the aim of semiology is to set up an appropriate position for language study. Or, semiology is kind of language oriented. So obviously, the foundation for interaction, interdependence, and interrelational constraints between linguistics and semiology has been long set. The combination of semiotics and linguistics is not only possible or practical but also sensible. (Wang Mingyu, "Linguistic Semiotics from the Semiotic Perspective" 8)

As we all know, Saussure takes two dimensions in studying language, synchronic and diachronic. In the former dimension, language is considered as a self-contained system whose interdependent parts function and acquire value through their relationship to the whole. From the perspective of signs, generic intertextuality can be understood as a kind of relationship among genres so as to put the study of generic intertextuality at a more macro level beyond discourse. At the same time, Saussure's diachronic view correlates with the dynamic and mixture and creation of genres, reflecting the idea of generic intertextuality.

Taking Saussure's view of language as semiotic, Peirce's approach to semiotic, and

Halliday's view of language as social semiotic, we are to distinguish genre from discourse and prove genre as macro social semiosis system by our analysis of language as well as its environmental semiotic system. Based on the view of genre as macro social semiosis system, generic intertextuality can be considered in essence as the relations among the components within the semiosis system. In this way, we try to construct a macro socio-semiotic rationale for generic intertextuality. Or our study in generic intertextuality is to be conducted under the theoretical background of macro social semiotics. Specifically speaking, we will borrow the distinction between system and process and apply it to the study of generic intertextuality, hence extending it to a higher level of application. And we will insist on the belief of generic intertextuality as the relations among the components within the macro social semiosis system of genre, putting an emphasis on semiosis as a sign process. Thus, the view of interaction and interpretation, a cognitive and newly understood sociocultural and interactive approach will be involved.

In this sense, generic intertextuality is a kind of system of resources, and underlies a dynamic process of interaction and cognition. Generally speaking, generic intertextuality which involves the interactive relation among semiotic processes of genre should be viewed in terms of semiotic systems of signification with ideology monitoring to offer an account of how particular combinations of register variables are culture-specific.

What's more, by taking the macro social semiotic view, our study manages to extend into a broader sense. "A social reality (or a culture) is itself an edifice of meanings — a semiotic construct". "In this perspective, language is one of the semiotic systems that constitute a culture; one that is distinctive in that it also serves as an encoding system for many of the others." (Halliday, *Language as Social Semiotic: The Social Interpretation of Language and Meaning* 2) That is to say, culture itself is an information system and needs to be interpreted in semiotic terms. It actually suggests that we should go beyond linguistics into social semiotics and take into account as many modalities of communication as we can systematically describe. (Martin and Rose 255) This is also true for our study in generic intertextuality. Multimodalities will be also involved in our study.

With the help of genre studies, we try to accomplish a comprehensive generic intertextuality system, which is to answer what are the potentials that we can choose from. And by referring to the space blending theory, we try to find the cognitive mechanism of generic intertextuality process, explaining how the potentials of generic intertextuality system can be chosen to realize the process of generic intertextuality or the configuration of generic intertextuality system. If our discussion of generic intertextuality process is about how the blending theory makes it possible to realize the cognitive mechanism of generic intertextuality, our discussion of generic intertextuality focus is to answer why this part of input spaces is mapped, not the others, or to answer why a subject chooses so, or what the motivation of the blending is. It is to be answered by reference to a theory of action. We assume that the key notion of intention in action theory controls the focus of generic intertextuality.

1.3 Aims and Objectives of the Study

In our dissertation, we insist on a multi-dimensional approach to our generic intertextuality study. According to van Dijk, there are three dimensions we should take in language research, language in use, delivery of beliefs or cognition and interaction in social contexts. (*Text and Context: Explorations in the Semantics and Pragmatics of Discourse* 2-4) The view has also been supported by what Halliday and Hasan state in *Language, Context, and Text: Aspects of Language in a Social-Semiotic Perspective*. In the normal course of life, all day and every day, when we are interacting with others through language, we are making inference from the situation to the text, about the kinds of meaning that are likely to be exchanged and also inferences from the text to the situation. (36) It implies three dimensions proposed by van Dijk. "Language in normal course of life" implies the dimension of language in use; "interacting with others" refers to the dimension of interaction in social contexts; and "making inferences" in both directions involves the dimension of exchange of beliefs or cognition. So, our study tries to build a comprehensive and multi-dimensional theoretical framework for generic intertextuality. Based on the multi-dimensional framework, we endeavor to achieve the following aims and objects.

Firstly, we try to construct a macro social semiotic rationale for studies in generic intertextuality. Within this theoretical framework, we try to distinguish genre from discourse. By taking genre as macro social semiosis system, we can define generic intertextuality more scientifically and make it possible to build a comprehensive and multi-dimensional theoretical framework for generic intertextuality which involves language in use, cognition and interaction.

Secondly, within the theoretical framework of macro social semiotic rationale, we try to give a systematic account of generic intertextuality resource system in the form of potentials. The potentials are assumed to be generalized according to the achievements from genre studies concerning both interaction and pragmatics. And in a broader sense, language is one of the semiotic systems that constitute a culture. The macro social semiotic perspective taken to define genre determines that generic intertextuality system must involve other possible modalities of communication. In other words, we are to go beyond linguistics into social semiotics and take into account many modalities of communication in our study in generic intertextuality.

Thirdly, we try to explore the cognitive mechanism behind generic intertextuality process or configuration of generic intertextuality. Since mental space theory, according to Fauconnier in his *Mental Spaces: Aspects of Meaning Construction in Natural Language*, is utilized to answer questions about the indirect reference and referential opacity and has been later proven to be useful to explain various linguistic and non-linguistic phenomena like math, gesture, music and creative design, we tend to apply it to our study in generic intertextuality. Through the application of space blending theory to explaining the cognitive mechanism of generic intertextuality process, we aim to answer how generic intertextuality process or configuration of generic intertextuality can be realized. It is emphasized that space blending occurs as an on-line and dynamic cognitive construction whose central process is conceptual blending. Some examples will be given to illustrate the central principles of the network model of conceptual integration for local purpose of thought and action. According to the theory, we are to prove there are at least four mental spaces participating in the genre space blending. They are input spaces, generic space and blended space by which some necessary conditions for blending are satisfied.

Fourthly, to work out a convincing explanation of cognitive mechanism of generic intertexutality, we are further to account for why this part of input spaces is mapped, not the others, or what the motivation of the blending is since a user conventionally focuses only on specific components from the whole set of resources. Specifically, we try to argue the process of generic intertextuality is ultimately determined by the function of a user's intention with the help of action theory. Furthermore, considering genre as a macro social semiosis system, we may well assume that ideology plays a very important role in determining a user's intention, and try to explore the role of ideology functioning on the focus. If the association between generic intertextuality and ideology can be proven, we are to further discuss what the carrier of ideology is and in what way ideology functions in generic intertextuality.

1.4 Organization of the Dissertation

We divide our dissertation into eight chapters. Chapter One is to give an overall introduction to our study. It briefs the origins of our study, illustrates the rationale of our study, makes clear the aims and objectives we try to achieve, and skeletons the outline of the dissertation.

Chapter Two presents a review of relevant theoretical background of generic intertextuality. In this chapter, some conclusive statements of achievements as well as deficiencies or limitations from former studies relevant to generic intertextuality are given.

Chapter Three is to construct a macro social semiotic framework for our study, in which genre is defined as macro social semiosis system and generic intertextuality is considered in essence as the relation of components within the semiosis system of genre. We try to show the reliability of applying the view of semiotics into generic intertextuality study and accomplish a comprehensive and multi-dimensional theoretical framework for our study in generic intertextuality.

From Chapter Four to Chapter Six, we respectively discuss generic intertextuality system, generic intertextuality process and generic intertextuality focus in detail. In Chapter Four, we try to illustrate the possible potentials as resources of generic intertexutality system. The potentials are disciplinary potentials, macro-speech act potentials, evaluation potentials, and modality potentials. By unveiling the resources for participants of generic intertextuality to choose from, we argue that when we talk about the intertextuality of a certain genre, we imply the reference of a certain component in a particular domain of potentials in generic intertextuality system. It is constant interaction across the domains of potentials that ensures generic intertextuality. And the components in each set of potentials are all organized hierarchically. That is to say, the combination of choices from each potential set realizes a genre. But some elements chosen from the potentials are not necessary but optional ones. They can be shared by other genres but not typical for a particular genre. When the essential elements of a certain genre are intertextualized, generic intertextuality occurs. So, studies in generic intertextuality can not only involve its system but also configuration of system or generic intertextuality process.

In Chapter Five, the mechanism for generic intertextuality process or how the choice from the potentials can be realized is to be focused on. The purpose of the chapter is to find the answer to the problems as to what the mechanism of the interaction or cognition of generic intertextuality process is, and how a subject can know what to choose from the resources and how to reorganize the information from the potentials to realize the process of generic intertextuality. Specifically, we first refer to the cognitive models for representations of the potentials, after which the mental models are further discussed. In this way, space blending theory is employed to explore the cognitive mechanism of generic intertextuality process.

Chapter Six looks into the motivation of blending, accounting for why a subject chooses so. According to an action theory, we try to argue the process of generic intertextuality is ultimately determined by the function of a user's intention. Furthermore, we try to discuss the role of ideology functioning on the focus and argue that there is always an interaction between ideology and generic intertextuality. Or, ideology and generic intertextuality are mutually influenced and interdependent.

Chapter Seven is devoted to the applications to English teaching. Some hints for English teaching we get from our generic intertextuality study are stated briefly. They are for the establishment of English teaching guideline, practical English teaching, role of teacher in class teaching and learning assessment.

The last chapter summarizes the major findings of our study. And, some limitations are listed and suggestions for further research are proposed.

Chapter Two

Literature Review

It has been argued that the origins of intertextuality should trace back to the Plato's theory of imitation which is the embryo of intertextuality. In the case of Platonic imitation, the "poet" always copies an earlier act of creation, which is itself already a copy. Actually, besides the theory of imitation, the magnetic image of charged interdependence, the passionate poet and reader and the notion of texts as subliminal purveyors of ideology are all the Plato's insights into the way texts function which have much in common with some modern theories of intertextuality. (Still and Worton 2—3) Since then, the notion of intertextuality has received a lot attention and been studied in different domains greatly. Generic intertextuality as a type of intertextuality is especially focused on since "a text cannot belong to no genre, it can not be without or less a genre". (qtd. in Miall 325) The discussion of generic intertextuality is talked about mostly in critical approach and in generic approach.

In this chapter, we will present a review of relevant theoretical background of generic intertextuality, giving some conclusive statements of achievements as well as deficiencies from former studies in generic intertextuality.

2.1 Origins of Intertextuality

2.1.1 Kristeva's Intertextuality in Text

The term of intertextuality is first coined by Julia Kristeva in *The Bounded Text*. Generally speaking, intertextuality means that "a text cannot exist as a hermetic or self-sufficient whole, and so does not function as a closed system". (Still and Worton 1) One of her most important contributions is to privilege the term of text. For her, all subjects are signifying systems which are composed by discourses. None of signifying systems is constituted in complete original manner but by intersection or transformation of earlier ones. A text must be understood in a dynamic sense. As she states, a text is a permutation of texts, an intertextulaity: in the space of a given text, several utterances, taken from other texts, interest and neutralized one another. (Kristeva, *Desire in*

Language 36) The interference of other texts can be an intersection of textual surfaces and a dialogue among the writer, the character and the contemporary or earlier cultural context. (Kristeva, *The Kristeva Reader* 36) Hence two dimensions of intertextuality can be achieved. One is the horizontal dimension to emphasize the close relationship between the producer and the interpreter. The other one is the vertical dimension to stress the connection of text and society or culture in history or in future.

It is worthwhile to emphasize that Kristeva highlights the social context. In line with Marxist sociology, Kristevan intertextuality suggests that meaning is not given nor produced by a transcendental ego. Indeed the transcendental ego is itself an effect produced in a social context. (Still and Worton 17) So in this sense, a text can never be considered as an isolated unit. Society and culture plays a necessary role in production and interpretation of text. The view of intertextuality in both horizontal dimension and vertical dimension is well presented in her own words as follows:

> Hence horizontal axis (subject-addressee) and vertical axis (text-context) coincide, bringing to light an important fact: each word (text) is an intersection of word (text) where at least one other word (text) can be read. In Bakhtin's work, these two axes, which he calls dialogue and ambivalence, are not clearly distinguished. Yet, what appears as a lack of rigour is in fact an insight first introduced into literary theory by Bakhtin: any text is constructed as a mosaic of quotations; any text is the absorption and transformation of another. The notion of intertextuality replaces that of intersubjectivity, and poetic language is read as at least double. (Ibid. 37)

It is obvious that Kristevan intertextuality is deeply influenced by Bakhtin's theories which closely follow Saussure's view of language. So, we will refer to Saussure's view of language.

2.1.2 Saussure's Implication for Intertextuality

Saussure has always been considered as the founder of modern linguistics. His linguistic theories are well shown in *Cours de linguistique générale* (*Course in General Linguistics*) which is compiled from the notes collected by his students on the lectures that he gave at the University of Geneva between 1906 and 1911 as well as his manuscripts left. The work has been thought epoch-making since the ideas in it extend great influences on the later development of linguistics and most contemporary structuralist thinking.

In the work, Saussure points out that language should be studied both in diachronically and synchronically. In other words, Saussure takes two dimensions in studying language, synchronic and diachronic. If we take the former dimension, language will be considered as a system of related items without reference to time. But the latter dimension leads us to focus on the evolutionary development of language over time. Saussure pays more attention to the synchronic studies and further divides language into two sides. By doing that, Saussure points out the differences among "langage", "parole" and "langue". The relation among them was presented by a diagram during his lectures as follows (Fig. 2.1):

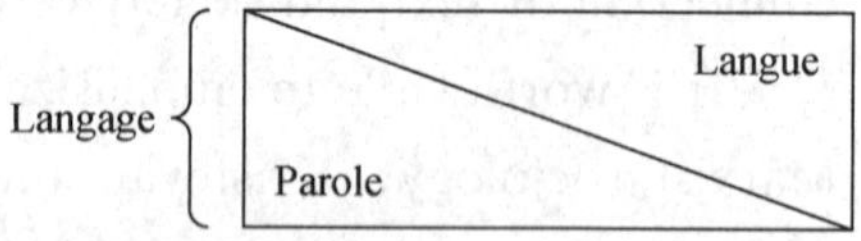

Fig. 2.1 A rational structure for the pursuit of linguistic studies (qtd. in Wang Mingyu, *Semiotic Linguistics* 17)

By the diagram, langage contains two respects including langue and parole. Langue, for Saussure, refers to the abstract system of signs consisting of the necessary set of linguistic rules that users of language must adhere to and parole is the practical utterances by particular language users with certain particular contexts or individual acts of speaking. Accordingly, langue is taken as the target we can study. Considering langue is a system of signs, it is possible to master the structure of langue and the system of meanings. Langue is an essential social product; while parole is accidental co-product of social conventions and individual linguistic abilities.

Since Saussure holds the belief that language is a system of signs expressing ideas, reasonably the basic elements of language for him are signs. Saussure manages to answer the question about linguistic signs. From a psychological perspective, a sign can be regarded as an entity with two sides, uniting the signified and the signifier. It implies that a language sign is the combination of concept (signified) and sound pattern (signifier). The model of sign can be shown in the following diagram (Fig. 2.2):

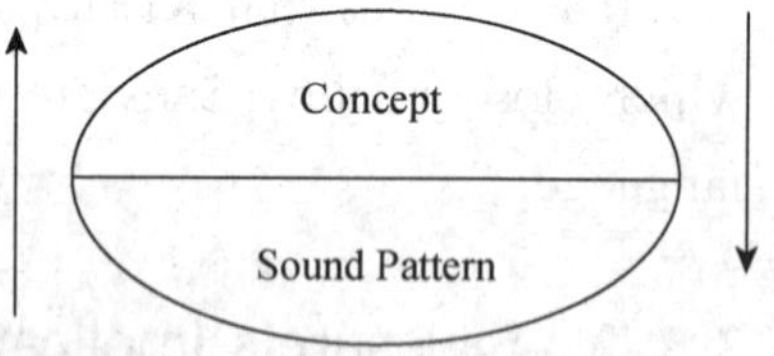

Fig. 2.2 Nature of the linguistic sign (Saussure 67)

Saussure does give explanation about sign in *Course in General Linguistics* to emphasize that language signs are not to refer to objects in the world. His explanation is as follows:

> A linguistic sign is not a link between a thing and a name, but between a concept and a sound pattern. The sound pattern is not actually a sound; for a sound is something physical. A sound pattern is the hearer's psychological impression of a sound, as given to him by the evidence of his senses. This sound pattern may be called a 'material' element only in that it is the representation of our sensory impressions. The sound pattern may thus be distinguished from other element associated with it in a linguistic sign. This other element is generally of a more abstract kind: the concept. (66)

On the basis of the view of the linguistic sign, Saussure further discusses the meanings of signs. The key principle of Saussure's idea about the meanings of sign lies in the arbitrary nature of the sign. It means that there is not a fixed relationship between the signifier and the signified. He proposes that signs are meaningful just because of their difference from other signs. Or the difference realizes the value of signs. Language is considered as a system of interdependent terms in which the value of each term results solely from the simultaneous presence of the others. Therefore, meanings of signs can only be achieved by relations. The meaning of a word exists only within a language system, only in differentiated relations to other words in that system. (Deacon 136) Then what is the relation among signs and how does the relation function? For Saussure, there are two kinds of relations among signs. On the one hand, within the language, words are connected in line. They can not occur at the same position and at the same moment. On the other hand, out of the language, some associated words are connected into a collection. Absent words in a certain collection may be substituted for those present in any particular linguistic sequence. Actually, this way is derived from the way in which signs are connected with one another in the memory. (Harris, *Saussure and his Interpreters* 124) Saussure introduces two concepts to refer to these two ways. The former one is of the syntagmatic orders of values in language; while the latter one is associative. According to Saussure, the principles of associative and syntagmatic ordering are evident at all levels of language. This ranges from the combination and association of different phonemes into words to the ordering of words into a sentences and discourse. (Howarth 22)

As to what the signified and the signifier mean respectively and as to what the relationship is between them for Saussure have been argued by various scholars. But it has been agreed that Saussure stresses the importance of sign system and relationship among signs. In other words, the non-referentialness and differentialness of language signs have been highlighted by Saussure. In some sense, it is the two properties of language signs that give birth to intertextuality. The theories of intertextuality share the idea that signs in a text do not refer to the objects in the world but the system out of which the text is produced. So the meaning of a text is not determined by the text itself but by its relation with the other texts. That is what we called as intertextuality. As Allen states, "texts, whether they be literary or non-literary, are viewed by modern theorists as lacking in any kind of independent meaning. They are what theorists now call intertextual. The act of reading, [...] plunges us into a network of textual relations. To interpret a text, to discover its meaning, or meanings, is to trace those relations." (1)

2.1.3 Bakhtin's Dialogism and Heteroglossia as Contributions to Intertextuality

Greatly influenced by Saussure, Bakhtin follows Saussure's fundamental ideas including that language is a system of signs and signs have the arbitrary nature. Instead of giving a clear definition of sign, he lists the properties of signs. Bakhtin insists that signs all have their substance base by which meanings are produced and signs must be involved in a certain period of history. Besides these, Bakhtin more emphasizes the important role of social context and ideology. For Bakhtin, sign is not a psychological entity and the meaning is not achieved by a psychological processing of signs. He pays more attention to the social context and holds the belief that the meanings of signs don't lie in the relation with other signs within abstract linguistic system but are realized in the social context. Different from Saussure's synchronic studies, Bakhtin highlights the historicity of signs. So generally speaking, Bakhtin holds a social and historical view rather than an individual and psychological view on language signs. As Vološinov whose publications are believed by some critics to have been authored by Bakhtin states, "language acquires life and historically evolves precisely here, in concrete verbal communication, and not in the abstract linguistic system of language forms, nor in the individual psyche of speakers". (95) In *The Formal Method in Literary Scholarship*, Bakhtin also writes that "not only the meaning of the utterance but also the very fact of its performance is of historical and social significance, as, in general, is the fact of its realization in the here and now, in given circumstances, at a certain historical moment, under the conditions of the given social situation. The very presence of the utterance is historically and socially significant." (120) Self-evidently, what Bakhtin focuses on is the "parole" rather than "langue". Hence utterances rather than sentences in his studies. Bakhtin does not challenges Saussure's idea of the arbitrary nature of language signs, but he proposes that besides sound pattern and concept there is another aspect we should consider about linguistic signs in use that is ideological meaning or evaluative accent. No utterances can be completely original and must be responses to others. As Bakhtin states as follows:

> When the listener perceives and understands the meaning (the language meaning) of speech, he simultaneously takes an active, responsive attitude toward it .... Any speaker is himself a respondent to a greater or lesser degree. He is not, after all, the first speaker, the one who disturbs the eternal silence of the universe. And he presupposes not only the existence of the language system he is using, but also the existence of preceding utterances — his own and others' — with which his given utterance enters into one kind of relation or another (builds on them, polemicizes with them, or simply presumes that they are already known to the listener). Any utterance

is a link in a very complexly organized chain of other utterances. (*Problem of Speech Genres* 124)

On this basis, Bakhtin gives his theory of language dialogism and his theory of two poles of literature, the monologic and the dialogic, which serve as Bakhtin's greatest contributions to intertextuality. Bakhtin argues that when people speak they use a specific mix of discourses which they have appropriated in an attempt to communicate their intentions. (Still and Worton 15) From the dialogical angle of discourse, the ideological intention of a speaker can both respond to the previous utterances and serve as the responded utterances for future ones. Therefore, "all utterances are dialogic, their meaning and logic dependent upon what has previously been said and on how they will be received by others." (Allen 19)

Utterances must be interfered with the various voices in certain social context. Every concrete utterance is intersected by both centrifugal and centripetal, unifying and disunifying forces. (Bakhtin, *The Dialogic Imagination* 272) That is to say, there can be monologism or poetry since writers attempt artificially to strip language of others' intentions; while there is much more possibilities that in a certain period of history writers tend to have the dialogic novel, creating heteroglossia. In his *Problems of Dostoevsky's Poetics*, Bakhtin argues it is impossible to read novels such as Dostoevsky's either as a homogeneous representation of reality, or as an expression of the author's personal opinions and psychology. Dostoevsky challenges his readers to recognize what Bakhtin calls the "polyphonic" novel, or that type of narrative which insists on the "coexistence and interaction" of very different ways of using language and, hence, very different ways of evaluating "reality". (qtd. in Thaïs Morgan 248) The idea of "polyphonic" novel is presented in his thesis "The Carnivalization of Literature". It is the carnivalistic attitude to reigning ideologies and the authoritarian institutions that distinguishes the polyphonic novel. As a matter of fact, "the notion of the carnivalization of literature, then, is nothing less than a theory of intertextuality, or the systematic connection that can be analyzed among literary and nonliterary discourses". (Ibid. 249)

Novels are enriched by social heteroglossia, by the historicity and social determination of specific languages, by the fact that words do not live in dictionaries but in other people's mouths. (qtd. in Still and Worton 16) So, although Bakhtin himself is never explicit about an application of anthropology and sociology to the literary semiotic, an interdisciplinary extension can be easily realized in his studies.

It is obvious that Bakhtin's concepts of dialogism and heteroglossia provide the prelude to the theory of intertextuality. Actually, the term of intertextuality proposed by

Kristeva directly stems from the idea of dialogism and heteroglossia. It can be well shown in her own words about intertextuality as follows:

> Each word (text) is an intersection of word (texts) where at least on other word (text) can be read. In Bakhtin's work, these two axes, which he calls dialogue and ambivalence, are not clearly distinguished. Yet, what appears as a lack of rigour is in fact an insight first introduced into literary theory by Bakhtin: any text is constructed as a mosaic of quotations; any text is the absorption and transformation of another. The notion of intertextuality replaces that of intersubjectivity, and poetic language is read as at least double. (Kristeva, *The Kristeva Reader* 37)

2.1.4 Barthes' Cryptogram as Intertextuality

Even before Kristeva's 1965 presentation of Bakhtin, Barthes was discussing the term of cryptogram which actually shares the same meaning of intertextuality. In *Writing Degree Zero*, he uses the term of cryptogram as follows:

> It is impossible to develop [my selected mode of writing] within duration without gradually becoming a prisoner of someone else's words and even of my own. A stubborn after-image, which comes from all the previous modes of writing and even from the past of my own, drowns the sound of my present words. Any written trace precipitates, as inside a chemical at first transparent, innocent and neutral, mere duration gradually reveals in suspension a whole past of increasing density, like a cryptogram. (qtd. in Still and Worton 19)

We believe that the term of cryptogram sharing the same meaning of intertextuality since both of them emphasize that any text must contain elements of other texts even it appears to be only its writer's own creative intentions. Barthes further proves his idea in *S/Z* where he locates some of the quotations without quotation marks in Balzac's *Sarrasine*, some of which refer to cultural codes, stereotypes and so on. As stated in the *Encyclopédie universalis*:

> The text is a productivity. Not in the sense that it is a product of being worked (as narrative technique or the mastery of style would demand), but as the very theatre of a production where the producer of the text and the reader come together: the text 'works' whenever and however it is taken up; even in written fixed for, the text does not stop working, or undertaking a process of production. The text deconstructs the language of communication, representation or expression [...] and reconstructs another language. [...] Every text is an intertext; other text are present within it to

> varying degrees and in more or less recognizable forms. [...] Every text is a new tissue of recycled citations. Fragments of codes, formulae, model rhythms, bits of social discourse pass into the text and are redistributed within it. [...] The intertext is a field of anonymous formulae whose origin is rarely recoverable, of unconscious or automatic citations without speech marks. (qtd. in Orr 33)

Later, in his work of *The Pleasure of the Text*, Barthes uses the term of "intertextuality" as "the impossibility of living outside the infinite text [...]; the book creates meaning, the meaning creates the life". (qtd. in Still and Worton 18) Here Barthes provides the term of intertextuality new interpretations. It means something more than the pleasure of picking up words (like "intertextuality" or "bourgeoisie") which have particularly seductive and / or complicated pasts; rather it explains that we make sense of our lived experience and hence construct our lives in relation to texts, whether these be Proust or television soap operas. (Ibid. 18—19)

Barthes is the most "perverse" of readers. For Barthes, the perverse reader is the reader who is a split subject. He is both of the consistency and the loss of the self. In *S/Z* "I" is a kind of intertextuality, a network of citations, and where each unit of reading functions, not by referring to a fixed content, but by activating certain codes in the reader. Accordingly, Barthes proposes the idea of death of the author, which implies his rejection of authority. It corresponds to the political thrust which Kristeva emphasizes in Bakhtin. But Barthes' use of the term bourgeoisie is both a citation from Marxist discourse and also, especially later, a link to aestheticism. Barthes seems ever ready to politicize seemingly natural matters of taste, but also to aestheticise seemingly political issues, since the theory of intertextuality denies the reality of power relations it can seem dangerously neutral. (Ibid. 21)

2.2 Developments of Intertextuality

2.2.1 Intertextuality in Applied Linguistics

Since the conception of intertextuality is raised, it has been studied in various fields from various perspectives. In the field of applied linguistics, Devitt studies the intertextuality in tax accounting from the social constructivist perspective. By exploring the range of the generic texts, she finds there is a genre set within a certain professional community. Take the tax accountants for example, though various tax accounting texts are produced with their own distinctive characteristics, we can locate the traces of interweaving with each other. It is intertextuality that connects the texts within the range of tax accounting. As stated, no text is single, as texts refer to one another, draw from on another, create the purpose for one another. (Devitt 336) Devitt associated genres with social community. For her, texts are the products of a particular social community, which present the community's epistemology and values. Furthermore, Devitt classifies intertextuality into three kinds. They are generic intertextuality, referential intertextuality and functional intertextuality

Another influential study from the social constructivist perspective is done by Bloome and Egan-Robertson. They define intertextuality as a social construction, located in the social interactions that people have with each other. (Bloome and Egan-Robertson 24) As to the social construction of intertextuality, three respects are involved. They are intertextual substance, intertextual processes, and intertextual rights. Since their study focuses on the intertextuality in classroom research and education, it provides a methodological view.

2.2.2 Intertextuality in the Systemic Functional Field

In the systemic functional field, the studies of interetextuality have been well done. In *Language, Context, and Text: Aspects of Language in a Social-semiotic Perspective*, Halliday and Hasan indicate that "the relationship between text and context is a dialectical one: the text creates the context as much as the context creates the text. Meaning arises from the friction between the two." (47) By the relationship, a set of previous text can serve as a part of the context for a text. Also from the systemic functional perspective, Lemke holds the belief that the meanings we make through texts, and the ways we make them, always depend on the currency in our communities of other texts we recognize as having certain definite kinds of relationships with them. ("Ideology, Intertextuality, and the Notion of Register" 275) On the basis of an additional set of criteria, he lists a number of ways intertextuality is realized or ways of intertextual references. They are as follow:

1. They can be generic (with genre membership as the basic criterion), e. g. reference to the 'committee meeting' genre.

2. They can be thematic or topical, e. g. reference to the bomb on Hiroshima.

3. They can be structural, displaying affinity of form, e. g. portmanteau words such as Reaganomics.

4. Finally, they can be functional, covering similarity in terms of goals, e. g. ways of saying 'I'm sorry'. (Ibid. 275)

Lemke gives us a relatively comprehensive understanding of intertextuality references, focusing on the relationships of meanings constructed between texts.

2.2.3 Intertextuality in Text Linguistics

There are some other influential linguists who carry the study of intertextuality. One of them is Beaugrande and Dressler in text linguistics. For Beaugrande and Dressler, intertextuality is one of seven standards of textuality. In *Introduction to Text Linguistics*, they discuss two respects of intertextuality. One is the relationship of a particular text to a type or genre. It means that our interpretation of any piece of writing must refer to the conventions it conforms to as a genre. The other respect is the relationship between particular texts, as described by Beaugrande and Dressler as text allusion. Generally speaking, Beaugrande and Dressler's classification of intertextuality only concerns the intertextual relationship at the level of texts, but not involves the higher level such as the intertextual relationship between genres.

Hamilton seems to have done intertextual studies in more global way. She explores intertextuality in conversation between herself and one Alzheimer's patient. By her interview analysis, she indicates the conception of intertextuality as the ways in which speakers/writers use language to establish and maintain ties between the current linguistic interaction (i.e., conversation) and prior ones involving the same participants, as well as the ways in which listeners/readers identify and use these ties to help them (re) construct a (the speaker's/writer's) meaning. (Hamilton 64) In some sense, Hamilton is to explore the intertextual relationships between different types of conversations or groups of conversations. Thus her exploration is in a more global way. However, her definition of intertextuality is too restricted probably because of her narrow exploration domain.

2.2.4 Intertextuality in Critical Discourse Analysis

In the linguistic field, another flourishing branch of intertextuality study is that in critical discourse analysis. As Xin Bin says, "the term critical is used here in the special sense of seeking to understand the relationships between ideas and their social conditions of possible existence and to show up connections which may be hidden from people, such as the connections between language, power and ideology". (*Intertextuality form a Critical Perspective* IX) Accordingly, the study of intertextuality in critical way focuses on the evolution of the ideological meaning of a text and to show both the influence on text from social structure and the influence on social ideology by text. In *Discourse and Social Change*, Fairclough gives a relatively comprehensive definition by viewing intertextuality from various angles as follows:

> Intertextuality is basically the property texts have of being full of snatches of other texts, which may be explicitly demarcated or merged in, and which the text may assimilate, contradict, ironically echo, and so forth. In terms of production, an intertextual perspective stresses the historicity of texts: how they always constitute additions to existing 'chains of speech communication' consisting of prior texts to which they respond. In terms of distribution, an intertextual perspective is helpful in exploring relatively stable networks which texts move along, undergoing predictable transformations as they shift from one text type to another (for instance, political speeches are often transformed into news reports). And in terms of consumption, an intertextual perspective is helpful in stressing that it is not just 'the text', not indeed just the texts that intertextually constitute it, that shape interpretation, but also those other texts which interpreters variably bring to the interpretation process. (84—85)

The most outstanding contribution Fairclough makes to intertextuality study is that he links intertextuality with power relations and believes that intertextuality is closely related with hegemony. According to Fairclough, the concept of intertextuality points to the productivity of texts, which is socially limited and constrained. The productivity can not be done by people with different social power equally. It is conditional upon relations of power. However, this kind of social limitations can be accounted for not only by the theory of intertextuality but also by referring to a theory of power relations. It is the combination of intertextuality and ideology and hegemony that is the starting point for Fairclough's research on intertextuality. In other words, he tries to introduce Foucault's idea of power relations into the understanding of intertextuality, hence bringing about a broader range of intertextuality exploration. Fairclough understands ideologies as significations or constructions of reality (the physical world, social relations, social identities), which are built into various dimensions of forms or meanings of discursive practices, and which contribute to the production, reproduction or transformation of relations of domination. (Ibid. 87) And hegemony, which is derived from Gramsci's analysis of western capitalism and revolutionary strategy in western Europe, is "leadership as much as domination across the economic, political, cultural and ideological domains of a society" and "the power over society as a whole of one of the fundamental economically-defined classes in alliance with other social forces, but it is never achieved more than partitially and temporarily, as an 'unstable equilibrium'". (Ibid. 92) So, when Fairclough links intertextuality with ideology and hegemony, he actually emphasizes the interaction between them. That is to say, discursive practice can well reflect hegemony while it is also a facet of hegemonic struggle which is much helpful to reproduce the existing order of discourse and that of existing social and power relations as well.

Furthermore, Fairclough holds that another significance of intertextuality is to lead to the ambivalence of texts. As stated in his own words, intertextuality is the source of much of the ambivalence of texts. If the surface of a text may be multiply determined by the various other texts which go into its composition, then elements of that textual surface may not be clearly placed in relation to the text's intertextual network, and their meaning may be ambivalent; different meanings may coexist, and it may be possible to determine "the" meaning. (*Discourse and Social Change* 104) In some sense, the ambivalence of texts can be understood as the dynamic of interpretation of a text as a result of intertextuality.

2.2.5 Summary

According to the achievements we briefed in various fields above, we may conclude that studies in intertextuality are not only to emphasize the importance of prior texts or the closely relevance to the former texts but also to highlight the contributions made by prior texts to a code which possibly renders the various effects of signification. Intertextuality should be considered as a designation of its participation in the discursive space of a culture. It implies that the study of intertextuality is not the investigation of sources and influences as traditionally conceived; it casts its net wider to include anonymous discursive practices, codes whose origins are lost, that make possible the signifying practices of later texts. (Culler 103)

In this sense, intertextuality can be a very complex and multi-dimensional concept. It is more significant to focus on how intertextuality can be accomplished rather than surface description of relationship among texts.

2.3 Generic Intertextuality as a Type of Intertextuality

2.3.1 Generic Intertextuality in Critical Approach

Generic intertexutality is proposed by Xin Bin in his *Intertextuality from a Critical Perspective*. It is a type of intertextuality distinguishing from specific intertextuality. For Xin Bin, generic intertextuality "is mainly concerned with current or historical relations between genres or types of discourse, each of which can be seen as presupposing a collective subject or a kind of addressees in the sense that each type of discourse is more or less in the monopoly of a social group, a class or an institution and different social sections are privileged by different discourse types". (*Intertextuality from a Critical Perspective* 93) Xin Bin takes the concept from the research of Fowler. According to Fowler, there is not a clear boarder among genres. A discourse can belong to a certain genre and bear the features of another genre at the same time. Since genres have to do with identifying and communicating rather than with defining and classifying, genre theory is properly concerned, in the main, with interpretation. It deals with principles of reconstruction and interpretation and (to some extent) evaluation of meaning. (Fowler, A. 38) For Fowler, the generic features within a discourse can be kind and can be mode. The terms for kinds, perhaps in keeping with their obvious external embodiment, can always be put in noun form, whereas modal terms tend to be adjectival. (Ibid. 88) For example, "a comic novel" means by kind a novel, by mode comic. The division between mode and kind reveals the phenomenon that a discourse of a certain genre can meanwhile carry the characteristics of other genres. It is what Xin Bin defines as generic intertextuality.

Xin Bin's classification of intertextuality is evidently influenced by the work of Fairclough. Fairclough draws a distinction between manifest intertextuality and interdiscursivity or constitutive intertextuality. For him, manifest intertextuality is a phenomenon in which other specific texts are overtly drawn upon within a text or "the heterogeneous constitution of texts out of specific other texts" (*Discourse and Social Change* 85); while interdiscursivity or constitutive intertextuality refers to "the heterogeneous constitution of texts out of elements of orders of discourse" (Ibid.) or "the configuration of discourse conventions that go into its production" (Ibid. 104).

Here, discourse convention can refer to a lot since Fairclough suggests the principle of interdiscursivity to apply at various levels including the social order of discourse, the institutional order of discourse, the discourse type, and even the elements which constitute discourse types. Fairclough holds that orders of discourse have primacy over particular types of discourse. Types of discourse are constituted as configurations of diverse elements of orders of discourse. Elements of orders of discourse can be possibly classified into types in widely-used terms as genre, style, register, and discourse. Fairclough's discussion of types of elements which make up orders of discourse are mainly genre, activity type, style, and discourse. That is to say, his concept of interdiscursivity is to involve genre, activity type, style and discourse. Fairclough assumes genre overarches the other types, in the sense that genres correspond closely to types of social practice, and the system of genres which obtains in a particular society at a particular time determines which combinations and configurations the other types occur in. (Ibid. 125) Genre is used by Fairclough to refer to a relatively stable set of conventions associated with a socially ratified type of activity and it implies dynamic processes of producing, distributing and consuming. In his *Analysing Discourse*, Fairclough further lists certain aspects of genres as follow:

1) The forms of action and interaction in social events are defined by its social practices and the ways in which they are networked together.

2) The social transformations of new capitalism can be seen as changes in the networking of social practices, and so change in the forms of action and interaction, which includes change in genres. Genre change is an important part of the transformations of new capitalism.

3) Some genres are relatively 'local' in scale, associated with relatively delimited network of social practices (eg. Within an organization such as a business). Others are specialized for relatively 'global' (inter) action across networks (genres of 'governance').

4) Change in genres is change in how different genres are combined together. New genres develop through combination of existing genres.

5) A chain of events may involve a chain or network of different, interconnected texts which manifest a 'chain' of different genres.

6) A particular text or interaction is not 'in' a particular genre — it is likely to involve a combination of different genres. (66)

According to the above aspects of genres, we can easily get the assumptions Fairclough makes in genre understanding. Firstly, genres have been associated with social events in the forms of action and interaction. Secondly, genres are open to changes and new genres are emerging by combination of existing genres. Thirdly, as to the relationship between genre and discourse, Fairclough concludes that genre analysis proceeds as analysis of genre mixtures in a particular text and individual genres in a particular text. As stated in his own words, genres are the specifically discoursal aspect of ways of acting and interacting in the course of social events: we might say that (inter) acting is never just discourse, but it is often mainly discourse. (*Analysing Discourse* 65)

Besides genre, Fairclough respectively explains other types of elements of orders of discourse including activity type, style and discourse and points out that the types rank on a scale from least to most autonomous. Activity is of least autonomy while discourse is of the most. According to Fairclough, activity type focuses on compositional structure or generic structure and can be specified in terms of the structured sequence of actions as well as the participants involved in the activity. Style is what a genre is always associated with, which varies according to the tenor, mode and rhetorical mode of the text. As the most autonomous of the types of element, discourse is traditionally discussed in terms of content, ideational meanings, topic, subject matter, and so forth. (*Discourse and Social Change* 128) On the basis of the ideas above, the interdiscursivity of a text is the mix of genres, styles and discourses.

To illustrate the idea of interdiscursivity, Fairclough gives an example of "A

Cardholder's Guide to Barclaycard". The text is as follows:

Using it's simple you don't even have to speak the language

Wherever you see a Visa sign you can present your Barclaycard when you wish to pay. The sales assistant will put your Card and sales voucher through an imprinter to record your name and account number.

He will then complete the voucher and after ensuring that the details are correct, you just sign it.

You'll receive a copy of the voucher, which you should keep for checking against your statement, and the goods are yours.

That's all there is to it.

You may use your Barclaycard as much as you wish, provided your payments are up to date and you keep within your available credit limit (this is printed on the folder containing your Barclaycard).

Occasionally the shop may have to make a telephone call to Barclaycard to obtain our authorization for a transaction. This is a routine requirement of our procedure, and we just make sure that everything is in order before giving the go-ahead.

In an effort to deal more quickly with these calls, Barclaycard is introducing a new automated system.

This will save time for you, but please note that any transactions which could take a Barclaycard account over its credit limit could well be declined.

It is important to ensure that your credit limit is sufficient to cover all your purchases and Cash Advances.

When you wish to take advantage of a mail order offer it's so much easier to give your Barclaycard number rather than sending cheques or postal orders.

Just write your card number in the space provided on the order form, sign it and send it off.

Or if you want to book theatre tickets, make travel reservations or even make a purchase by telephone, just quote your card number and the cost can be charged to your Barclaycard account.

You'll find Barclaycard can make life a whole lot easier. (Ibid. 114)

In the example, a new genre of information - and-publicity emerges by mixing the genre of financial regulations and the genre of advertising. Since a genre implies not only a particular text types, but also particular processes of producing, distributing and consuming texts (Ibid. 126), the interdiscursivity can be reflected by the producers' functioning in two situations and two sets of subject positions. On one hand, the bank is to inform regulations; on the other hand, the bank is to sell the card. When the two functions and two sets of subject positions mix, a new genre is created.

Both of Fairclough and Xin Bin try to make a distinction between two types of intertextuality and explore them in critical way. And ideological transmission is the key problem for generic intertextuality.

2.3.2 Generic Intertextuality in Generic Approach

In the domain of genre studies, there is a debate between generic integrity and creation of new genres. The view of generic integrity holds that genre is a rhetorically situated and highly institutionalized textual activity, while the other view assigns genre a property of innovation and change, which is often exploited by the expert members of the specialist community to create new forms in order to respond to novel rhetorical contexts or to convey "private intentions within the socially recognized communicative purposes". (Bhatia, *Worlds of Written Discourse* 24) The former view seems to focus on typical identifiable and ideal discourses of genres. But in the real world, it is always true that members of a professional community can manipulate and exploit generic resources to respond new emerging rhetorical contexts. Discourse is self-evidently complex, dynamic, constantly developing and often less predictable. Most often genres in real world are seen in hybrid, mixed and embedded forms. The dynamic and mixture of genres well reflect the idea of intertextuality. As a matter of fact, in the domain of genre studies, the property of generic intertextuality has been realized and discussed in diverse ways. In 1987, by modifying his former assertion of genre, Kress focused the dynamic of genres. His statement is as follows:

> Genres are dynamic, responding to the dynamics of other parts of social systems. Hence genres change historically; hence new genres emerge over time and hence, too, what appears as 'the same' generic form at one level has recognizable distinct forms in differing social groups. (qtd. in McCarthy and Carter 32)

Kress's idea actually echoes the view held by new rhetoric. The new rhetorical tradition presented by Miller, Bazerman, Freedman and Huckin all hold that texts are dynamic cultural presentation and genres are dynamic and historical. As Campbell and Jamieson show that a genre is composed of a constellation of recognizable forms bound together by an internal dynamic. ("Form and Genre in Rhetorical Criticism: an Introduction" 21) Thus, genre is considered as dynamic and unstable entities, generic forms are flexible and the number of genres is indeterminate.

The idea of dynamic shares a lot in common with Bakhtin's view in his *The Problem of Speech Genres*. As Bakhtin states, "utterances and their types, that is, speech genres, are the drive belts from the history of society to the history of language". (123) When it comes to the complexity of genres, Bakhtin proposes that utterances are not indifferent to one another and they are aware of and mutually reflect one another. In some sense, it is the response to the other utterances that determines the dynamic and complexity of genres. What's more, genres do come from the response to other genres. A new genre is always the transformation of an earlier one, or of several: by inversion, by displacement, by combination. (Todorov 15) That is to say, although any text must be of genre, it can never belong to only one genre. The generic intertextuality or the heterogeneity of genres is always in any text. Many linguists have proven it by their own researches.

For example, Devitt lists thirteen genres of tax accounting, which form a genre set. Each genre in the set reflects a different rhetorical situation which in turn reflects a different combination of circumstances that the tax accountant repeatedly encounters. (Devitt 340) Self-evidently, it seems necessary to understand the other genres in the set if you want to understand one genre. What Devitt discusses is the tax accounting genre set, but generic intertextuality is not confined to tax accounting field only. It can be applied to all fields of texts, literary or nonliterary.

According to Swales, the genre set refers to a particular individual — or more often a class of individuals — engaged in, either or both receptively and productively, as part of his or her normal occupational or institutional practice. Swales even gives an example of genre set as graduate students move through the system. So all genres mix together and no hard boarder among them. Since most genre studies highlight the communicative purpose of a genre, it has been explained that the invasion of the integrity of a genre and the creation of a hybrid form are to fulfill more complicated communicative purposes.

Some other concepts sharing the similar meaning of genre set have been proposed, such as Swales' genre network, Bazerman's system of genres and Bhatia's genre colony. They all refer to the phenomenon of invasion of the integrity of one genre by another or genre convention, often leading to the creation of a hybrid form. (Bhatia, *Worlds of Written Discourses* 58) They all bring in the key Bakhtinian notion of intertextuality, bearing the view that the use of earlier generic forms, or the use of the linguistic and rhetorical features associated with those genres, to strengthen or modify the genre exemplar under construction. (*Research Genres* 21)

Take an advertisement introduced by Bhatia for example. The advertisement is as follows:

OVERHEARD AT FANLING GOLF COURSE

1st PLAYER: "How was your trip to Indonesia?"

2nd PLAYER: "Great. Got all the business done ... and got in a spot of golf."

1st PLAYER: "Hear business isi booming there?"

2nd PLAYER: "Yes. We're very optimistic about the future, so we're opening an office in Jakarta next month."

1st PLAYER: "I thought you liked Indinesia?"

2nd PLAYER: "I do. I have invested in the Barclays Indonesia Fund. It's up 66% over the past three years *."

1st PLAYER: "Sounds good. Know anyone there?"

2nd PLAYER: "Call my contact at Barclays, Sarah Robbins, on 8261988, or your investment advise can help."

1st PLAYER: "Thanks. I'll follow it up. By the way, you just played my ball!"

* Source Micropal 01/010/94

Dear Sarah,

I recently heard about the great performance of the Barclays Indonesia Fund. Please send me information on how I too can benefit from Barclays' Asia expertise with as little as US$1,500. My business card is enclosed.

BARCLAYS

Level 16, two Pacific Place, 88 Queensway, Hong Kong

It must be remembered that the value of shares and income from them can decrease as well as increase and the past performance figures are not indicative of future performance.

(qtd. in Bhatia, *Worlds of Written Discourses* 80)

The advertisement is a text with two genres mixed. One is dialogue and the other is letter. But it is still an advertisement. It is the mixture of genres that makes it more attractive.

So, to settle the debate on the tension between generic integrity and the possibility of using generic resources to create new genres in the field of genre studies, the idea of generic intertextuality seems an effective way.

2.3.3 Summary

Both in critical approach and generic approach, the importance of generic intertextuality has been highlighted. But different schools of scholars have different theoretical concerns and explore intertextuality of genres in their particular fields or from some specific perspectives relevant to their own fields. Accordingly, the delimitation of generic intertextuality is still far from definite and studies in generic intertextuality are not satisfactory. And some deficiencies or limitations in former studies are unavoidable. They are as follow.

First of all, the former studies in generic intertextuality are more a kind of descriptive study rather than explanatory fully or deeply enough, although the communicative purposes have been concerned. The formal features or linguistic representations of generic intertextuality are paid more attention, while the deeply causes of generic intertextuality have been less involved. In the former studies in generic intertextuality, a less addressed issue is how the producers and receivers in a particular discourse community to do with other intertextualized discourses when generic intertextuality occurs. Both generic and critical approaches talk about what generic intertextuality looks like or a little bit why it is there. Especially in genre theory, there has often been an overwhelming emphasis on the analysis of linguistic resources, with very little attempting to integrate the socio-cognitive factors that so often contribute to the act of genre construction, interpretation, use and exploitation to achieve non-linguistic ends in real life. (Bhatia, *Words of Written Discourse* 112) No cognitive mechanism of generic intertextuality concerning how generic intertextuality happens has been involved. But it probably is an area worth further research.

Secondly, when we talk about the interdiscursive character of a text being realized in semantic, grammatical and lexical features of the text, we actually explore generic intertextuality at the level of discourse rather than group of discourses or genre. Interdiscursivity concerns genres or mix of genres, but only configuration of genre or discourse since every discourse must be of genre. According to Fairclough, interdiscursivity refers to the mix of genres, styles, activity types and discourses. Diverse elements of orders of discourse which can be possibly classified into types in terms as genre, style, register, and discourse are all involved in Fairclough's discussion of interdiscursivity. Thus, we may well suggest the necessity of constructing a more macro rationale to distinguish genre, style, register and discourse. In this way, the difference between Fairclough's interdiscursivity and generic intertextuality can be clarified and a more definite understanding and sensible delimitation of generic intertextuality can be achieved.

Thirdly, since the elements of orders of discourse are extremely diverse and it is by no means always easy to decide whether one is dealing with genres, styles, discourses, or whatever, there is not and could not be, a determinate list of genres, styles or discourses, and it often appears to be rather arbitrary decisions about whether something is or is not a separate instance of one of these types. (Fairclough, *Discourse and Social*

Change 125) So in some sense, the lack of established terminology for genres, styles and discourse types hinders the exploration of generic intertextuality. That is to say, we can refer to the studies in generic properties to explore the generic intertextuality and distinguish the difference between generic intertextuality and interdiscursivity. The combination of the generic approach and the critical approaches is necessary.

Fourthly, it is true that the studies in generic intertextuality in critical approach have proposed that generic intertextuality is developed from the social ideology, and the closely relationship between generic intertextuality and ideology has been well accepted. However, the studies are only conducted within the domain of critical linguistics or from the perspective of critical approach. No further details about any operable linkage between them are explored. We have not got full ideas about how to realize the association between generic intertextuality and ideology, or what the carrier of ideology is and in what way ideology functions in generic intertextuality.

Last but not least, the theoretical basis for generic intertextuality seems not convincing or sensible enough. Studies in generic intertextuality are variously conducted based on different theoretical assumptions. Each rationale for any study to base on is partly convincing and sensible since it only concerns one perspective or dimension of generic intertextuality. In some sense, it is the lack of inclusive and powerful rationale that results in some of limitations mentioned above.

However, although studies in generic intertextuality in both critical approach and generic approach have some limitations, generic intertexutality has been explored in some sensible ways in both of them. The critical approach shows the importance of ideology implied in the process of intertextulaity of genre; while the generic approach unveils the importance of generic intertextuality in the genre theory by analyzing the natures and functions of genres. So in some sense, the critical approach and the generic approach make contributions to the research of generic intertextuality by showing us the orientation of exploration.

Conclusively speaking, we can surely do more to make up the limitations in former studies, on the basis of the achievements from former studies and even employing some practical ways applied in former studies. The research of generic intertextuality should start from the discussion of natural properties of genre so as to possibly delimitate the concept of generic intertextuality and to decide what are involved in generic intertextuality. To improve former studies in generic intertextuality, we need a more global rationale to study generic intertextuality. Genres are to be considered above rather than at the level of discourse. Not only the formal features but also the cognitive mechanism of generic intertextulaity should be explored since the cognitive mechanism of generic intertextuality plays a necessary role in a comprehensive study in generic intertextuality. And ideologies or social and historical views are also expected to be involved. All in all, we need a more comprehensive theoretical framework to explore generic intertextuality in a multi-dimension way.

Chapter Three

Theoretical Framework Construction

As we have mentioned above, we need a more comprehensive framework to talk about generic intertextuality so as to improve former studies in generic intertextuality. Our to-be-constructed framework also borrows some valuable achievements from former studies. Specifically speaking, our study is based on the understanding of genre properties and criteria. We hold a belief that the comprehensive understanding of genre will help a lot to achieve a working definition of generic intertextuality for our present study. So in this section, we start with sketching out the influential genre studies so as to reveal the natural properties of genre.

The generic properties and criteria determine that a study in generic intertextuality must be conducted in a socio-semiotic orientation at a macro level. Thus, we try to construct a macro socio-semiotic rationale for generic intertextuality. Taking partially Saussure's view of language as social semiotic, Peirce's approach to semiotic, and Halliday's view of language as social semiotic, we are to distinguish genre from discourse and prove genre as macro social semiosis system by our analysis of language as well as its environmental semiotic system.

Then we will try to further apply partly Peirce's approach and the views of Saussure as well as his followers such as Halliday to the study of generic intertextuality. Specifically speaking, we will borrow Saussure's distinction between system and process and apply it to our study in generic intertextuality, hence extending it to a higher level of application. And we will partly follow the Peirce's emphasis on semiosis as a process and his view of interaction and interpretation, thus, the cognitive and the newly understood sociocultural and interactive approach will also be involved.

Based on the view of genre as semiosis system, generic intertextuality can be considered in essence as the relations of components within the semiosis system of genre. In this sense, generic intertextuality is a kind of system of resources, and underlines a dynamic process of interaction and cognition. Generally speaking, generic intertextuality involving the interactive relation among semiotic processes of genres should be viewed in terms of semiotic systems of signification with ideology monitoring to offer an account of how particular combinations of register variables are culture-specific.

To fulfill a relatively comprehensive theoretical framework, we emphasize a lot the interaction and cognition of generic intertextuality represented by generic intertextuality process, as well as the motivation of a particular process which is shown as focus in our theoretical construction.

3.1 Delimitation of Generic Intertextuality

3.1.1 Overview of Genre Studies

The term of genre is most attractive but extremely slippery. Genres have aroused most attention but been considered as one of the least defined areas in linguistics. Far in the illustrious history of the discipline, not so much as one genre has been completely defined. (qtd. in Swales, *Genre Analysis* 34) For one thing, the importance of genres has been well realized as a means of constructing and interpreting discourses and even a necessary tool to understand the world. As Hawkes contends that a world without a theory of genre is unthinkable, and untrue to experience. (101) For another, although interpretations of genre originate and are abound in literature, it may be fair to say that there has not been a satisfactory theory of genre in the field of literature. A study of genre must be on the basis of achievements from a variety of academic disciplines such as literary studies, rhetoric, sociology, psychology and applied linguistics, etc. The diversity of approaches motivated by different orientations in genre study determines the complexity of the nature of genre. Different people can understand the concept of genre and study genres in different ways. However, any understandings and studies in genre have their origins and are influenced by the research achievements in some fields. Thus, we think it necessary to review and sketch some theories which give great influences on the development of genre studies.

We may have another term to share the similar meaning of genre — style. The study of style is traditionally regarded as stylistics that is defined as "a branch of linguistics which studies the characteristics of situationally-distinctive uses of language, with particular reference to literary language, and tries to establish principles capable of accounting for the particular choices made by individuals and social groups in their use of language" in *The Fontana Dictionary of Modern Thought*. (qtd. in Thornborrow and Wareing 3)

From the definition we can see that the study of style is still about linguistics but focuses on literary texts. The western stylistics originated in rhetoric. The publication of *Traité de stylistigue française* by Bally in 1909 signaled the spring-up of stylistics. Until the 1960s stylistics was established as a discipline. In the 1960s and 1970, stylistics reached its prosperous stage with the focus on form and function. In the 1980s, the study of style turned to the conversation analysis with an emphasis on the interactive process between communicators. In the 1990s, the flourish of stylistics in the sense of social culture led to the stress on the ideology implied in style. Nowadays, the trend of stylistics is multi-discipline oriented and more schools of stylistics are being formed. According to *A Dictionary of Stylistics*, "the study of style; [...] just as style can be viewed in several ways, so there are several different stylistic approaches. This variety in stylistics is due to the main influences of linguistics and literary criticism [...]" Thus, it is obvious that style has a lot in common with genre and the achievements in the field of stylistics may well lead us to believe that the characteristics of users of styles, whether the individuals or the social groups, are more concerned with. It now serves as a part of genre study, or tends to be associated with it, as suggested by Roger Fowler's definition of genre that it refers to a set of texts with recognizable formal and stylistic similarities, which relates to some common communication situation. (227)

3.1.2 Origins of Genre Studies

Genre study can be traced back over two thousand years ago. Aristotle first classified literary texts into three categories including poetry, novel and drama. Because of his classification of literary texts, genre is defined as a distinctive type or category of literary composition as glossed by *Webster's Third*. (Swales, *Genre Analysis* 33) This kind of definition can be well supported by Freedman and Medway's description of genre. "Genre has been viewed as: (a) primarily literary, (b) entirely defined by textual regularities in form and content, (c) fixed and immutable, and (d) classifiable into neat and mutually exclusive categories and subcategories." (1)

Although the context of literary was later expanded to include discourses of any type, spoken or written, with or without literary aspirations, the term of genre has been for a long time used to refer to a distinctive category of discourses in various fields. Actually ever since Aristotle, rhetorical inquiry and criticism has been interested in classifying discourse, one common approach has been to proceed deductively, in a top-down manner, and construct a closed system of categories. (Ibid. 42) A typical example is Kinneavy's classification of discourse into four main types: expressive, persuasive, literary and referential. What's more, in folklore studies one of perspectives taken by some scholars such as Linnaeus is also to consider genre as a classificatory category. In their opinions, a story can be classified as a myth, legend or tale. This classificatory work is to consider genres as ideal types but actual texts usually deviate from the ideal in various ways. Rather than considering genre as a classificatory category, other folklorists see genres as permanent forms. As Ben-Amos stated, "they have an independent literary integrity, which withstands social variations and technological developments." (qtd. in Swales, *Genre Analysis* 34) A similar stress on the form of genre can be found in some genre study by rhetorical scholars with an inductive orientation. As Campbell and Jamieson said:

> A genre is a group of acts unified by a constellation of forms that recurs in each of its members. These forms, in isolation, appear in other discourses. What is distinctive about the acts in a genre is a recurrence of the forms together in constellation. (20)

So generally speaking, genre study begins in the literary domain. The traditional concept of genre somewhat focuses on the classification and form. However, genre study is not only derived from the literary classification but also from some contributions of cultural anthropology and the philosophy of language.

It has been well known that after the 1950s the structurism ended its dominant role in the linguistic field. It was challenged greatly by the Chomskyan theory, generally known as the transformational generative grammar, with his book of *Syntactic Structures* published in 1957. According to the Chomskyan theory, any linguistic behavior can be governed by a set of rules stored in the human minds and people have underlying awareness of the rules of his language. That is to say, if we can find the universal rules about how to organize the constituents into grammatically correct sentences, we can easily analyze language via form only and in complete isolation. The Chomskyan theory was so popular and influential that was considered as the mainstream of linguistics in those years. But the Chomskyan theory has often been criticized for its neglecting the situational and contextual study of language and failing to treat language as language in use. With the development of Functional Grammar, more and more linguists began to integrate the study of language with its situation and context. The functional orientation owes a lot to the contributions of anthropology, sociology and the philosophy of language.

The concept of context was first proposed by Malinowski in the anthropological settings. By observing the daily life and events of the residents on Trobriand Islands, Malinowski found it impossible to understand a language without particular context. The particular context was first identical with context of situation within which a language was used. And later, Malinowski further developed his idea of situational context into cultural context and argued that there was a certain relation between language and culture. The view of context of situation and context of culture has been inherited and further developed by Firth into a theory of meaning. The Malinowski-Firth tradition is generally known as the "British contextualism". It is the British contextualism that greatly influences the work of systemic functional linguists. It is the Malinowski's view of language as a kind of social activity with context of culture that has much influence on the ethnography of communication. So, the significance of Malinowski's work not only lies in the view of context but also in the perception of language as a means to realize social activity.

The similar proposal can be found in the philosophy of language. The philosopher John Austin suggested the premise that every utterance can be understood as the speaker's intention to achieve a specific purpose in his famous *How to Do Things with Words*. The premise implies any speech does more than what its proposition means. Any speech can be regarded as an act. Hence, speech act theory was set up. Speech act theory has been widely used in various studies of language usage, just as Levinson claims that "of all the issues in the general theory of language usage, speech act theory has probably aroused the widest interest". (226)

Conclusively speaking, there are two key points we can get from anthropology and the philosophy of language. One is the ideas of contexts of situation and culture. The other one is the perception of language as speech act. These two origins influence the later genre studies a lot. In linguistics, for example, Saville-Troike takes genre to refer to the type of communicative event; Hymes holds that genres often coincide with speech events; (Hymes, *Foundations in Sociolinguistics* 61) Hallidayean linguists regard genre as the staged purposeful social processes through which a culture is realized in a language. (Martin and Rothery 243) In rhetoric, Miller argues that a rhetorically sound definition of genre must be centered not on the substance or form of discourse but on the action it is used to accomplish. (151) In literary studies, both Todorov and Fowler accept that genres are coded and keyed events set within social communicative processes. (qtd. in Swales, *Genre Analysis* 38)

3.1.3 Properties of Genre

The theoretical origins discussed above in some sense show us the basis of the later genre studies. Or the later genre studies in various domains mostly develop from one of these theoretical origins according to their different theoretical concerns and address different questions in their particular field. For example, since the emergence of the concept of cultural context, genre has closely linked with society and culture. In the domain of literature, Dubrow, Hauptmeier and Reid all prove the importance of context in interpretation. The ethnography of communication which is based on anthropology and linguistics is also primarily concerned with the description and analysis of the social context in which a linguistic interaction occurs. In this section, we try to sketch some of the influential and representative genre theories which have been proposed by different schools and scholars from different perspectives, by which properties of genre can be generalized, not only traditional properties such as genres as families and prototypes, genres as language standards, but also some more developed ones.

3.1.3.1 Genre of Dynamic as Communicative Event

Ever since Aristotle, genre has been considered to be in the domain of literature and has widely been discussed in literary theory. The definition of genre in much of current literary theory has been principally through the work of Bakhtin. And Bakhtin is the first person who extended the genre study into the non-literary domain. In his *The Problem of Speech Genres*, Bakhtin points out that "literary genres have been studied more than anything else. But from antiquity to the present, they have been studied in terms of their specific literary and artistic features, [...] and not as specific types of utterances distinct from other types, [...] The general linguistic problem of the utterance and its types has hardly been considered at all". (122) He further indicates that

> language is realized in the form of individual concrete utterances (oral and written) by participants in the various areas of human activity. ... Each separate utterance is individual, of course, but each sphere in which language is used develops its own relatively stable types of these utterances. These we may call speech genres." (121)

Thus, Bakhtin holds the view of dynamic genre and believes that the meanings we make about a text are based on certain situational background.

Working within the field of ethnography of communication, Hymes defines genre as one of components by which the speech event is identified, which implies that genres often coincide with speech events. But he further points out that genres must be treated as analytically independent of speech events. They may occur in or as different events. The sermon as a genre is typically identified with a certain place in a church service, but its properties may be invoked, for serious or humorous effect, in other situations. (*Foundations in Sociolinguistics* 61) As for speech event itself, it "will be restricted to activities, or aspects of activities, that are directly governed by rules or norms for the use of speech". (Ibid. 52) Although Hymes distinguishes genre from speech event, he still highlights the close relationship between genre and context.

3.1.3.2 Genre with Purpose Realized by Structure in Discourse Community

There are some other scholars who identify genre with speech event. The most influential one may be Swales. He gives a definition of genre as follows:

> A genre comprises a class of communicative events, the members of which share some set of communicative purposes. The purposes are recognized by the expert members of the parent discourse community, and thereby constitute the rationale for the genre. This rationale shapes the schematic structure of the discourse and influences and constrains choice of content and style. Communicative purpose is both a privileged criterion and one that operates to keep the scope of a genre as here conceived narrowly focused on comparable rhetorical action. In addition to purpose, exemplars of a genre exhibit various patterns of similarity in terms of structure, style, content and intended audience. If all high probability expectations are realized, the exemplar will be viewed as prototypical by the parent discourse community. The genre names inherited and produced by discourse communities and imported by others constitute valuable ethnographic communication, but typically need further validation. (*Genre Analysis* 58)

In Swales' definition, three concepts are focused on. They are "communicative purpose", "schematic structure", and "discourse community". By the definition, Swales suggests that communicative purpose determines genre and provides structure of genre. Discourse community is the ownership of genre. To further support his idea, Swales proposes the concepts of moves and steps in constructing a text. For example, a Create a Research Space (CARS) model with moves and steps is given as follows (Fig. 3.1):

Move 1 Establishing a territory Step 1 Claiming centrality and/or Step 2 Making topic generalization(s) and/or Step 3 Reviewing items of previous research	↓ Declining rhetorical effort
Move 2 Establishing a niche Step 1A Counter-claiming or Step 1B Indicating a gap or Step 1C Question-raising or Step 1D Continuing a tradition	↓ Weakening knowledge claims
Move 3 Occupying the niche Step 1A Outlining purposes or Step 1B Announcing present research Step 2 Announcing principal findings Step 3 Indicating RA structure	↓ Increasing explicitness

Fig. 3.1 A CARS model for article introductions (Ibid. 141)

From the figure we can see that the development from move 1 to move 3 is accompanied with increasing explicitness and weakening knowledge claims. Therefore, with the help of moves and steps, article introduction can be more easily followed by readers.

Greatly influenced by Swales' work, another practitioner of English for Specific Purposes (ESP) Bhatia gives his definition also centering on "communicative purpose", "conventionalized internal structure" and "discourse community". He defines genre as

> A recognizable communicative event characterized by a set of communicative purpose(s) identified and mutually understood by the members of the professional or academic community in which it regularly occurs. Most often it is highly structured and conventionalized with constraints on allowable contributions in terms of their intent, positioning, form and functional value. These constraints, however, are often exploited by the expert members of the discourse community to achieve private intentions within the framework of socially recognized purpose(s). (*Analyzing Genre* 13)

Working in the same field, other practitioners of English for Specific Purposes (ESP), such as Dudley-Evans, Paré and Smart, Bazerman and Myers, all stress the close relationship between genre and discourse community, and the importance of communicative purpose in genre identification and internal structure realization.

The defining effect of the social purpose and schematic structure for a genre is also acknowledged by the systemic linguists. For Martin and Rose, "a genre is a staged, goal-oriented social process. Social because we participate in genres with other people; goal-oriented because we use genres to get things done; staged because it usually takes us a few steps to reach our goals". (7—8) Actually, greatly influenced by Halliday's systemic-functional linguistics and Bakhtin's work on genre, Martin interprets context as two communication planes, genre and register, so as to get a three plane model of language (as shown in Fig. 3. 2) and distinguish the difference between genre and register. Register functions as the expression form of genre, at the same time language functions as the expression form of register. Thus, genre is to concentrate on the integration of meanings engendered by field, tenor and mode as systemically related social processes. (Martin, *English Text: System and Structure* 495)

Register involving field, tenor and mode is realized by contextual configuration which is described by Hasan as a specific set of values. According to Hasan, by contextual configuration we can predict the structure of a text. Since CC (contextual configuration) is an account of the significant attributes of this social activity, it is not surprising that the features of the CC can be used for making certain kinds of predictions

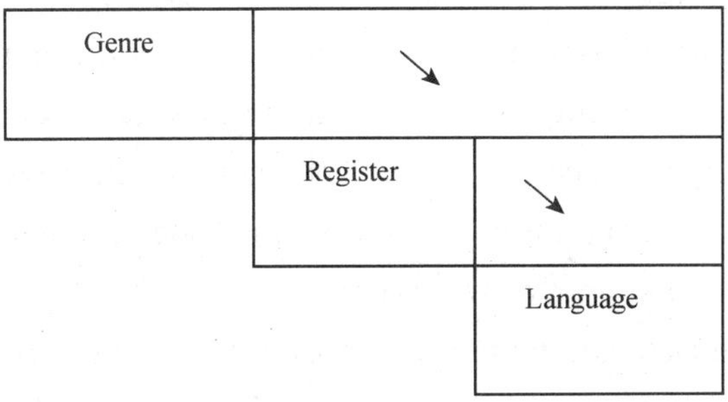

Fig. 3.2 Stratifying context as language's content plane (Ibid.)

about text structure. (Halliday and Hasan, *Language, Context and Text: Aspects of Language in a Social-semantic Perspective* 56) The structure of text is expressed in term of generic structure, or in Martin's words, the schematic structure of a particular genre.

Still in the field of systemic functional linguistics, for Eggins and Slade, a genre is staged as the meanings are made in steps, it usually takes more than one step for participants to achieve their goals; a genre is goal oriented in that texts typically move through stages to a point of closure, and are considered incomplete if the culmination is not reached; genre is negotiated interactively and is the realization of a social purpose. (56)

The view of social purpose in genre is also held by new rhetoricians. In *Genre as Social Action*, Miller also indicates that genre should be defined by the action it tends to accomplish not by the substance or the form.

3.1.3.3 Genre of Cognitive Nature

The definitions of genre have been continuously modified, even in the works of the same scholar. More than ten years after Swales shows his definition of genre in *Genre Analysis*, Swales advances the understanding of genre. He takes genres as metaphors. Specifically speaking, genre does not only involve linguistic form, but also involves frames of social action, language standards, biological species, families and prototypes, institutions and speech acts. His idea can be described as follows (Fig. 3.3):

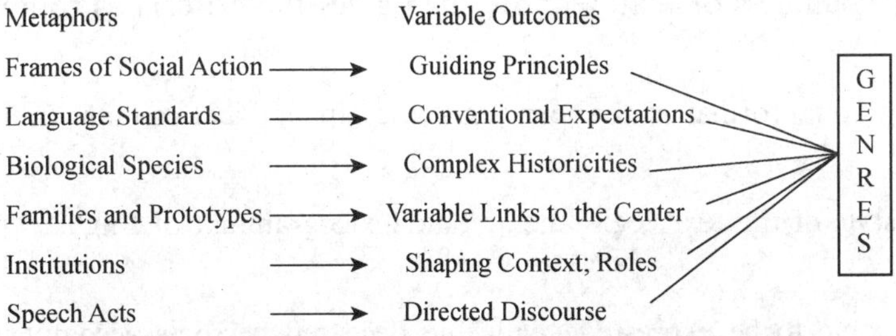

Fig. 3.3 Swales' metaphors of genres (*Research Genres* 68)

Besides the traditionally understood natures of genre, Swales adds the sense of cognition into the definition. Actually, the sense of cognition in genre understanding has been proposed before. According to what Bhatia argues in "A Genre-based Approach to ESP Materials", there is an aspect concerning the cognitive and psychological structuring of genres we should focus on in genre study and one of the four aspects of genre acquisition is sensitivity to cognitive structures.

In Berkenkotter and Huckin's views, genres are "dynamic rhetorical forms that are developed from actors' responses to recurrent situations and that serve to stabilize experience and give it coherence and meaning". And meanwhile, "genres change over time in response to their users' sociocognitive needs". So genre knowledge is "a form of situated cognition that continues to develop", revealing "a discourse community's norms, epistemology, ideology and social ontology". (4) As Johns argues from a pedagogical perspective, genre is "complex, evolving mental abstractions held by individuals within communities or larger cultures who share social and textual experiences". (22)

The cognitive property of genre has been long before proposed in folklore studies. The Russian formalist Propp whose monograph gives much inspiration to further develop a story grammar argues that the meaning of a text comes from the relationships among the elements of a text, which in turn implies a deeply cognitive structure of a genre. Furthermore, when Ben-Amos treats genres as ideal types, he associates genres with conceptual categories of communication.

3.1.4 Criteria for Genre Decision

As to the criteria to distinguish genres for a text from the others, properties of genre play determining roles and different scholars hold different views. Take Johnstone's view for instance, he insists that we need to describe the form of texts of the genre; the contexts in which the genre is relevant, in which participants may use genre to organize, explain what they are doing and why; the activities by which people create and share the knowledge required to produce texts in the genre; and how the genre works in interaction. (158) However, Beaugrande believes it is impossible for genres to prescribe specific rules or boundless of features. He then gives the criteria as follows:

1) the graphic format of the text (eg., the alphabetical columns in a "telephone directory");

2) the style of the text (eg., the archaic lexicogrammar of English "psalms" and "prayer");

3) the topic to be expressed (eg., the deceased person's accomplishments and virtues for the "eulogy" at a funeral);

4) the participants who are likely or entitled to produce the text (eg., the drill instructor who gives the "orders" in the Marine Corps);

5) the plan and goal (eg., seeking a buyer for your "used automobile" through a "classified ad");

6) the situation in which the type occurs (eg., a job interview calling for a "resumé");

7) the informativity suitable to participants (eg., a "training lecture" for electronicians to operate and service a new machine);

8) the institution that codifies the type and defines the participants (eg., a criminal court where you enter a "plea");

9) the medium of presentation (eg., a telephone answering machine to present a recorded "greeting" and to request a "message" after a "beep").

(*New Foundations for a Science of Text and Discourse* 314—316)

Beaugrande tries to embrace all the possible factors determining a genre, including formal features, styles, contents, participants, purposes, context, media and so on. But obviously, they can not be complete. In reality, a genre is always determined by selective criteria and combination of criteria, which leads to the difficulty of getting a closed and definite generic system. That is probably why Beaugrande holds the view of uncontrollable generic complexity.

To handle out the complexity of criteria of genre, some linguists try to make a distinction between genre and text type. It is commonly accepted that genre is a kind of type with external or non-linguistic criteria while text type with internal or linguistic criteria. (Hu Shuzhong, *Studies in English Textlinguistics* 171) The distinction successfully classify the elements of factors influencing genre. Actually, in most of genre studies, the criteria of genre have been non-linguistic or external. And the division of genre and text type has been applied in genre studies.

Genre theories in various fields seem to cover the different orientations. But if we give a more closely look at them, we can get a lot of common grounds which come from the natural properties of genre. Some of grounds have been summarized by Bhatia on the basis of the analysis of the studies of situated linguistic behaviors. They are as follow:

1) Genres are recognizable communicative events, characterized by a set of communicative purposes identified and mutually understood by members of the professional or academic community in which they regularly occur.

2) Genres are highly structured and conventionalized constructs, with constraints on allowable contributions not only in terms of the intentions one would like to give expression to and the shape they often take, but also in terms often lexico-grammatical

resources one can employ to give discoursal values to such formal features.

3) Established members of a particular professional community will have a much greater knowledge and understanding of the use and exploitation of genres than those who are apprentices, new members or outsiders.

4) Although genres are viewed as conventionalized constructs, expert members of the disciplinary and professional communities often exploit generic resources to express not only 'private' but also organizational intentions within the constructs of 'socially recognized communicative purposes'.

5) Genres are reflections of disciplinary and organizational cultures, and in that sense, they focus on social actions embedded within disciplinary, professional and other institutional practices.

6) All disciplinary and professional genres have integrity of their own, which is often identified with reference to a combination of textual, discursive and contextual factors.

(*Worlds of Written Discourse* 23)

Bhatia's summarization involves some fundamental properties of genre. And according to these realized properties, he gives a definition of genre as "language use in a conventionalized communicative setting in order to give expression to a specific set of communicative goals of a disciplinary or social institution, which give rise to stable structural forms by imposing constrains on the use of lexico-grammatical as well as discoursal resources". (Ibid.) Meanwhile, Bhatia points out that genre is not static so as to reveal the dynamic of genre. The dynamic of genre can be specified with genre's continuous development and change, the exploitation of new textualization patterns, the hybrid and mixed and embedded forms of genres. Accordingly, the concept of system of genres is proposed.

Conclusively, the discussion of the notion of genre which is diverse among theorists shows the necessity of interdisciplinary study in genre to achieve a more comprehensive understanding of genre. The most important perceptions of genre can be generalized as follow: (a) genre is social and cultural in nature, hence the association with ideology; (b) genre is a kind of goal-oriented communicative events; (c) genre is an activity involving a group of participants in a certain community; (d) genre is social-cognitive; (e) genre is dynamic.

3.1.5 A Working Definition of Generic Intertextuality

Although it is widely argued that generic integrity is important for most perspectives on genre, the dynamic of genre caused by generic intertextuality is highlighted. Generic intertextuality has been defined as a type of intertextuality compared with specific intertextuality. In critical approach, Xin Bin holds that generic intertextuality is to analyze a text as a play of voices of different utterances made from shifting positions specified by the genres that the text invokes. (*Intertextuality from a Critical Perspective* 191) Although the notion of generic intertextuality and the notion of interdiscursivity are differentiated as interdiscursivity focuses both on blends of discursive formations and blends of genres, Xin Bin just substitutes interdiscursivity with generic intertextuality without maintaining a clear distinction between blends of discursive formations and blends of genres. By applying the distinction made by Fowler between kind and mode, Xin Bin set his definition of generic intertextuality. In his words, generic intertextuality is the mixture of styles, registers and genres.

Our definition of generic intertextuality differs a little from Xin Bin's. Firstly, as we talk above, style can be partially considered as genre in our study, or what style concerns should be concerned in genre study. What's more, according to Martin's model of contexts, register serves as expression plane of genre and corresponds to the situational contexts in the part of cultural context in Halliday's model. But in Kress's view, register can be divided into several types. They are dialect, genre, mode, discourse, plot, character and report, narrative, and so on. The division can be shown as follows (Fig. 3.4):

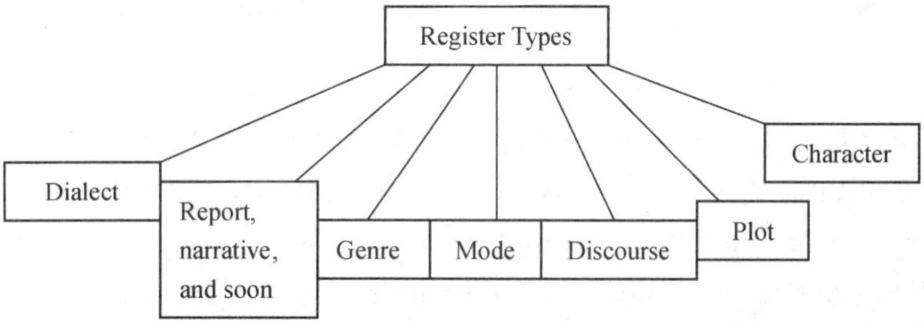

Fig. 3.4 Kress's division of register (qtd. in Hu Shuzhong, *Studies in English Textlinguistics* 171)

Both of the views about register are to prove the closely relationship between register and genre. As to whether genre is content plane of register or genre is a type of register, we hold an opinion that register is about discourse or configuration of genre, while genre is about types of discourse. Thus, as Genette argues that we should approach intertextuality and the other kinds of transtextuality through the larger units of discourse and genre analysis. (qtd. in Thaïs Morgan 267) The construction of framework about generic intertextuality should be more concerned with genre, including the properties of genre and criteria of genre. And the generic properties and criteria discussed above determine that a study in generic intertextuality must be conducted in a socio-semiotic orientation at a macro level.

As we have discussed above, genre differs from text type as genre takes the external or non-linguistic criteria. To claim sufficient expertise in genre intertextuality, we may well need to understand the aspects of text-external criteria which involve socio-cognitive. According to Bhatia, the text-external indicators of generic integrity are respectively shown in diagrams as follows (Fig. 3.5):

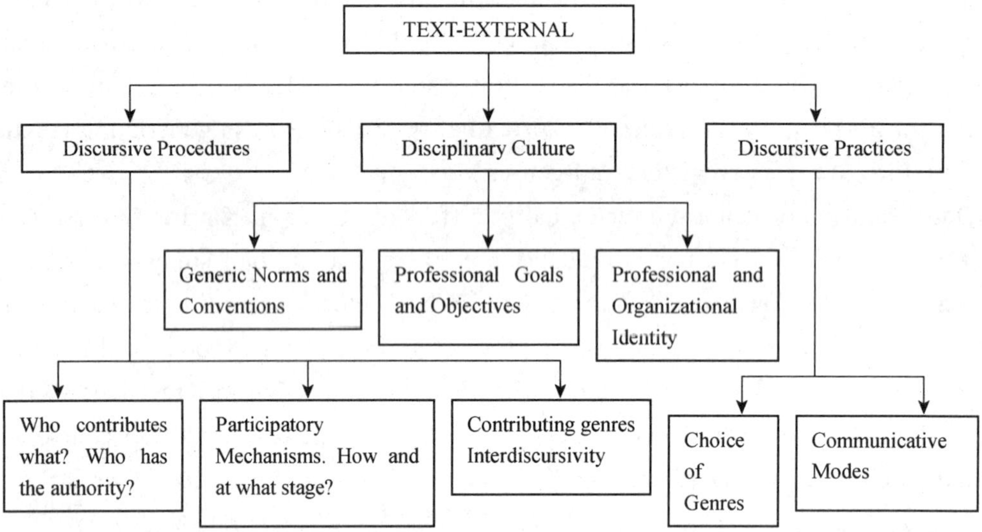

Fig. 3.5 The text-external indicators of generic integrity (*Worlds of Written Discourse* 127)

According to the diagram above, there are three types of text-external factors about genre identification. They are discursive practices, discursive procedures and disciplinary or professional culture. And Bhatia gives detailed explanation about each of them.

Discursive practice includes information about the choice of appropriate genres as well as knowledge about what modes of communication are appropriate to what kind of professional action. Generally speaking, discursive practice is to answer the questions as what kinds of genres are used, what modes of communication are employed and what organizational constraints operate on these practices.

Discursive procedures constrain the procedural aspects of genre construction, including how to construct, interpret, use and exploit genres, who are the participants in the genre construction activity, who have the authority to contribute what to the construction of specific genres, how the participatory mechanism works and who takes control at which stage of the process.

The last type of disciplinary culture specifically includes professional goals and objectives, generic norms and conventions, and professional and organizational identity. In the subset, the to-be-settled questions more focus on institutional concerns.

We take the view that genres and text types are different and genres' criteria should be text-external, and we hold a belief that the construction of framework about generic intertextuality should be at a macro level, that is, be based on understanding of genre. Thus, we have our working definition of generic intertextuality according to the text-external criteria and properties of genre as well.

Generic intertextuality refers to the blends of genres, productivity and permutation of genre, determined by variables of generic criteria. It not only involves discursive practice but also discursive procedures and disciplinary cultures. In each of them, both product of generic intertextuality and procedure of generic intertextuality are concerned, which include social cognitive, social culture and social participation.

In this sense, our study takes a comprehensive perspective, not only concerning what generic intertextuality looks like in a specific discourse or focusing on the configuration of generic intertextuality but also trying to explore why and how it is realized. Furthermore, since our study distinguishes generic intertextuality from discoursal intertextuality and understands genre as macro socio-semiotic, we try to put our study at a macro level and from a socio-semiotic perspective.

3.2 Macro Socio-Semiotic Rationale Construction

3.2.1 Language as Semiotic Resource System

3.2.1.1 Saussure's Language as Social Semiotic

In the famous book *Course in General Linguistics*, Saussure says,

> It is therefore possible to conceive of a science which studies the role of signs as part of social life. It would form part of social psychology, and hence of general psychology. We shall call it semiology (from the Greek smeon, 'sign'). It would investigate the nature of signs and the laws governing them. Since it does not yet exist, one cannot say for certain that it will exist. But it has a right to exist, a place ready for it in advance. Linguistics is only one branch of this general science. The laws which semiology will discover will be laws applicable in linguistics, and linguistics will thus be assigned to a clearly defined place in the field of human knowledge. (15—16)

The words above reveal the aim of Saussure's semiology that is to set up an appropriate position for language study. Linguistics should be a branch of semiology since language in nature is a system of signs. Or for Saussure, semiology is language oriented.

As we have discussed in Chapter One, Saussure takes two dimensions in studying language, synchronic and diachronic. If we take the former dimension, language is considered as a self-contained system whose interdependent parts function and acquire value through their relationship to the whole. The synchronic dimension refers to no time, while the diachronic dimension focuses on the evolutionary development of language over time. Saussure pays more attention to the synchronic study in language and further divides language into langue and parole. Thus, language for Saussure can contain two respects including langue and parole.

Langue, for Saussure, refers to the abstract system of signs consisting of the necessary set of linguistic rules that users of language must adhere to, which leads to the possibility to master the structure of langue and the system of meanings. Accordingly, langue is the target we are able to study. It is in his discussion of langue that Saussure proposes the concept of system of signs. As a system of signs, langue should share some inner characteristics in common within it. They are the arbitrary nature of the sign, the social nature of the sign, the psychological nature of the sign, the continuity nature of the sign and the changeable nature of the sign. When it comes to the social nature of the sign, Saussure argues that "language never exists apart from the social fact, for it is a semiological phenomenon". (77) In general, language is a social fact, or language is an essential social product. What does Saussure mean by social product or social fact? The answer lies in his explanation of the arbitrary nature of signs. When Saussure talks about the arbitrary nature of signs, he emphasizes that people can never use any signifiers for any signified randomly since they must follow the rules of a certain community. In his own words, "the signifier, though to all appearances freely chosen with respect to the idea that it represents, is fixed, not free, with respect to the linguistic community that uses it". (71) In some sense, the relative restraint of signs proves the social nature of language.

Actually the division of langue and parole helps a lot to distinguish what is social and what is individual. Since society knows language as a product inherited from preceding generations and accepted as such, language has been regarded as a kind of social fact. According to Sampson, a social fact is a conception in the collective mind which is there beyond the individual and reflected partially in the minds of members of a certain community. So Saussure's view of language as social semiotic is in contrast with that of speaking as an individual act. And the concept of social semiotic is to further support his explanation of langue as a system of signs. Although Saussure's concern with questions of meaning and signification not only prompted investigation into the nature of language itself, but also resulted in the extension of linguistic models into the social sciences more generally (Howarth 16), the concept of social semiotic is nothing to do with how social factors influence language and use of language.

What's more, the nature of signs held by Saussure reveals that language as a system of signs is a kind of network system of relations. Saussure uses "value" to generalize two kinds of relations which serve as two aspects of linguistic value. On the one hand, the concept appears to be just the counterpart of a sound pattern, as one constituent part of a linguistic sign. One the other hand, since language is a system in which all the elements fit together, the value of any one element must depend on the simultaneous coexistence of all the others. (Saussure 113) Two kinds of relations are later developed into two kinds of comparison, associative and syntagmatic which are used to restrict the relation among elements in the system of language. It sets a relatively arbitrary relation among them so as to make it possible to orderly arrange linguistic signs and form a structural whole. That is why we think Saussure's view of language as semiotic is a kind of structural view.

3.2.1.2 Peirce's Approach to Semiotic

The origin of modern semiotics can be traced back to two great persons — Saussure and Peirce — who are respected as the founders of modern semiotics. They in the same period propose the science of semiotic. Furthermore, Peirce's philosophy has always been considered as a main stream of modern philosophical school which greatly influences the development of modern semiotic. So it seems necessary to review Peirce's approach to semiotic as well as his view of language as semiotic.

Peirce takes a broad view of signs. With a semiotic approach to all kinds of activities, Peirce takes semiotics out of the narrow confines of linguistic sign. Peirce holds that, in society, we are surrounded by signs of various descriptions, which is the essence of human interaction. Unlike de Saussure, Charles Peirce's approach stems from pragmaticism. It is the pragmaticism that leads to some essential ideas in Peirce's approach. In contrast of Saussure's model of sign in the form of a self-contained dyad or dyadic relation, Peirce treats the sign as a triadic unity with representamen, object, and interpretant. And he offers a triadic model. It determines a triadic relation in a sign as Hatim and Mason say:

> 1) Whatever initiates identification of the sign.
>
> 2) The object of the sign.
>
> 3) The interpretant or the effect the sign is meant to relay. Generally speaking, the interpretant may be regarded as the meaning of the sign. (109)

The interpretant is the key to show the most important difference between Saussure's approach and Peirce's approach. As Saussure takes any linguistic entity only in virtue of the association between signal and signification, he neglects the process of transformation. Saussure's association does not involve the relation between sign and object or the relation between sign and interpretant. It seems in no way to realize the transformation from sign to object or from one sign to another. But Peirce does. He proposes a medium to bring a subject into the process of sign and introduce perception, interpretation and cognition into it. In this sense, a kind of association is set up by interpretant, and sign can serve as a passing way from idea to reality. That is why Peirce insists that anything can be considered as sign only when it is interpreted as sign. Thus, a process of sign lies in the triadic relation in which a "representamen" arouses an interpretation about an object in an interpretant's mind. It is actually a cognitive process that happens in an interpretant. This relation can be indicated as follows (Fig. 3.6):

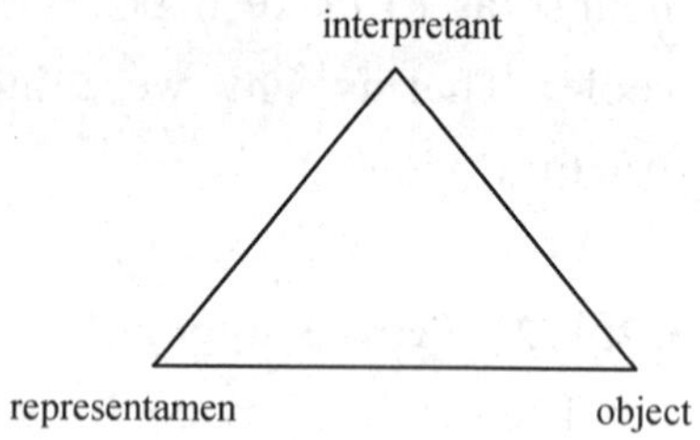

Fig. 3.6 Peirce's process of a sign (qtd. in Li, Qiaolan 117)

What's more, in the Peirce's understanding of process of sign, he further proposes the unlimited semiosis which plays another key role in his approach. Within it, Peirce's "interpretant" may be seen as having the quality of endless commutability. In other words, interpretant can constantly assume ever-wider meanings. Peirce points out that not only representamen and object but also interpretant are all signs. Thus the interpretant itself will arouse the more developed interpretation. Again, the more developed interpretant triggers the more and more developed interpretation. It continues endlessly, since all interpretants can be signs. The process can be shown in Fig. 3.7.

It is in this way that cultural beliefs are sustained. Indeed, whole myths can develop as a result. They may span centuries and cross generations, thus helping to define the value systems of entire cultures. (Hatim and Mason 112)

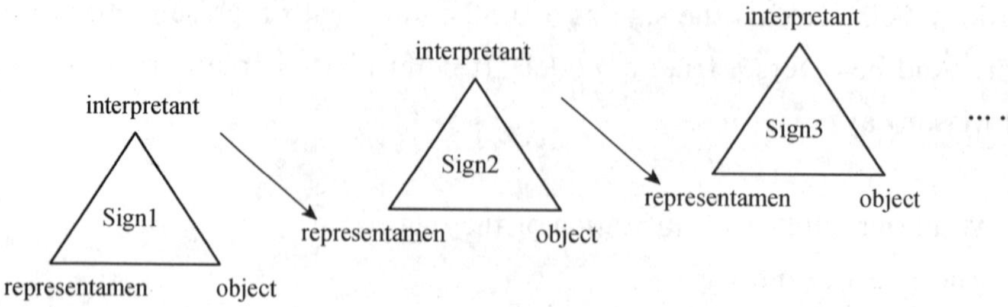

Fig. 3.7 The process of signs (qtd. in Li, Qiaolan 117)

Self-evidently, interpretant is the key as well as the link in the endless process of sign. First of all, it is interpretant that brings interpretation or meanings to sign, and associates representamen with object. So the meanings of signs must be realized by interpretation which involves a cognitive process. Secondly, the endless process makes the interpretation of sign complicated since a sign can be interpreted not only within the sign but can be interpreted by the sign outside of the sign which has been interpreted in the former process of sign. For example, a board with words of "Keep Silence" outside of a classroom as a sign can be interpreted in the first semiotic process as "no talking" or "don't be noisy". And it can be further interpreted in the more developed process as students are taking examination or having a lecture. The idea of endless process of sign determines that the use of sign must be dependent on the former experiences of sign uses. And it causes the dynamic of process. The process of sign is a dynamic process within a subject in cognitive practice or between subjects in communicative practice. In different situations and by different subjects, sign can be interpreted differently. Anyway, cognition is the key in the process.

Thus, for Peirce,

> A sign ... [in the form of a *representamen*] is something which stands to somebody for something in some respect or capacity. It addresses somebody, that is, creates in the mind or that person and equivalent sign, or perhaps a more developed sign. That sign which it creates I call the *interpretant* of the first sign. The sign stands for something, its *object*. It stands for that object, not in all respects, but in reference to a sort of idea, which I have sometimes called the *ground* of the represnetamen. (qtd. in Daniel Chandler 32—33)

What Peirce studies on sign in a broader way surely influences his view of language. Pierce takes process of linguistic sign as dynamic, interactive and cognitive. The process of linguistic sign is a kind of dynamic interaction between subjects in communicative practice. And the dynamic interaction must be realized by subjects' cognitive practice since it stresses the importance of the active process of interpretation and rejects the equation of content or meaning. In this sense, the dynamic interaction can be identical with subjective interaction. (Deely 23) As Parmentier argues that interaction here shares much in common with Bakhtin's dialogism which is regarded as an origin of intertextuality. And the interaction is operated by cognition. After all, language is concerned as highly conventional symbolic sign which can be interpreted according to a rule or a habitual connection. "The symbol is connected with its object by virtue of the idea of the symbol-using mind, without which no such connection would exist". (qtd. in Chandler 38)

If we try to find the counterpart of Saussure's sign in the language system, it may be the word or more specifically the sound pattern. The meaning of a word as a sign is produced by the combination of its signifier and signified. And the value of sign is determined by the relationship between the sign and other signs within the system as a whole. Hence the language structure at various levels is used to express any meanings or propositions in the world. While in the Peirce's approach, the sign itself is a unity of proposition representing any meaning in the world. Applied to language, the unity of sign is discourse. The process of sign is the process of cognition involving interpretant.

However, the subject involved in the process of sign is not a social subject but a biological subject. The man who participates in any semiotic activity carries no social marks but is only a biological individual.

3.2.1.3 Halliday's Language as Social Semiotic

For much of the past twenty years, linguistics has been dominated by an individualist ideology, which explicitly banished all reference to the social context of language. It seems that nearly every sentence uttered is uttered for the first time. The grammar of this kind of linguistics is a set of rules; and the conceptual framework is drawn from logic. The typical representative of this kind of linguistics is Chomsky who reduces the natural language to a formal system. For him, language can be analyzed into ordered rules. And what's more, after his emphases changed during the 1960s, he takes the grammar of language not as an abstract descriptive system or a product of the linguist's analysis any longer but as a property of one's cognition. Thus, Chomsky is much interested in the internal structure of man's brain, the biological nature. Specifically speaking, in terms of the capacity of human brain, language is considered as knowledge. In this way, Chomsky's theory of language is a kind of formal, structuralist account of an abstract system completely cut off from communicative interaction. But self-evidently, any communicative phenomenon can not always be explained by the set rules, especially when language users are involved. The ultimate core of language communication does concern the exchange of meanings which usually takes place in particular contexts. Accordingly, the interpretation of language is dynamic and the exchange of meanings is creative.

Based on the belief that the process of exchange is creative, Halliday argues that language is one of symbolic resources used to exchange meanings. It is in this perspective that the grammar of linguistics is about choices rather than rules. And the choices will be done according to the functions serving in life. In order to understand them in this way we have to proceed from the outside inwards, interpreting language by reference to its place in the social process, (Halliday, *Language as Social Semiotic: The Social Interpretation of Language and Meaning* 4) or take an inter-organism perspective to take language as behavior. Thus, language is taken as an encoder of a "behavior potential" into a "meaning potential". It is to turn what a man "can do" into what he "can mean".

It is Halliday who develops the theory of language as social semiotic successfully. As

Halliday says, "a social reality (or a 'culture') is itself an edifice of meanings — a semiotic construct". "In this perspective, language is one of the semiotic systems that constitute a culture". (Ibid. 2) In this sense, language is interpreted within a sociocultural context, while the social structure or system and culture are interpreted in semiotic terms as an information system.

In Halliday's systemic functional grammar, social contexts can be classified into three types in which meanings are exchanged. They are tenor determined by the social groups and communication networks, field constituted by the types of social activity, and mode involving the rhetorical channel with its associated strategies. All of them originate in the social structure. Furthermore, from a social perspective, SFG is to believe that there are certain functions which must be fulfilled in all human cultures, regardless of differences in the physical and material environment. These metafunctions are what we know as ideational function, interpersonal function, and textual function, which are built into the semantic system of language.

In terms of realization, the semantic system of language realizes the behavioral system, or the semiotic system of social context, which is figured out in Fig. 3.8. That is to say, the semantic system is an interface between linguistic system and higher symbolic system of social context.

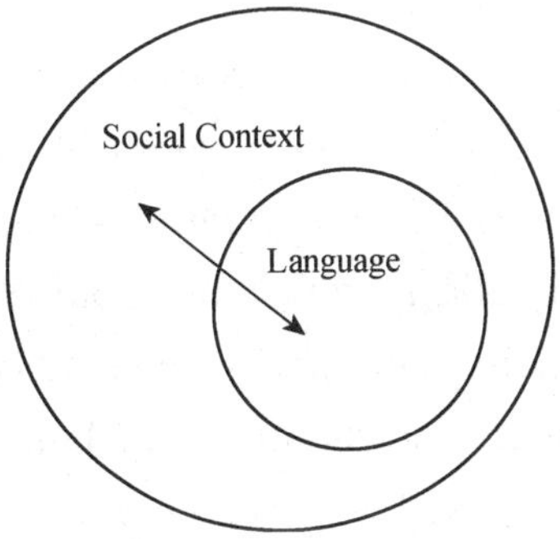

Fig. 3.8 Language as the realization of context (Halliday and Marin 25)

In this sense, the social system is interpreted as a social semiotic system: a system of meanings that constitutes the reality of the culture. The meaning potential of language, which is realized in the lexicogrammatical system, realizes meanings of a higher order; not only the semiotic of the particular social context, its organization as field, tenor and mode, but also that of the total set of social contexts that constitutes the social system. (Halliday, *Language as Social Semiotic: The Social Interpretation of Language and Meaning* 123—124)

3.2.1.4 Summary

In its broadest sense, semiotics comprises all forms of formation and exchange of meaning on the basis of phenomena which have been coded as signs. (Johansen and Larsen 3) Language which is considered as a system of signs has been argued a lot about its social nature. But the view of language as social semiotic says very little by itself since it can be interpreted differently in different frameworks. Up to now, we have introduced some of influential interpretations about it with the purpose of founding a theoretical basis for our further construction of macro socio-semiotic rationale.

Although Saussure's sign system is different from Peirce's semiosis or sign process, they are not contradictory but complementary. They just take the different perspectives to study signs, which greatly influences their own view of language. Saussure stresses the systematic relationship between linguistic signs. His focus is on language as the prototypical system which is collective and governed by internalized rules used well-nigh unconsciously and is in several important ways built just like a purposely planned system such as traffic signs. (Ibid. 48) Although Peirce takes all linguistic signs as symbols and thus characterizes them in terms of their conventionality in a similar way to Saussure, he introduces the interpretant and emphasizes the cognition in the sign process. The cognition is nothing about society but biological individual. So, the characteristics of Saussure's view of language are its social and systemic or structural characteristics; while those of Peirce's approach determine his view of language as cognitive and interactive, and bring the dynamic into language communication. It is even fair to say, in some sense, Peirce's approach may well be the basis of cognitive involvement in linguistics and pragmatics. (Guo, Hong 15)

Halliday is greatly influenced by Saussure, but his conception of language as social semiotic is different from Saussure's. Halliday's "social" is not in contrast with "individual" but in contrast with "psychophysiological". For Halliday, if we are to understand the nature of language, it is necessary to consider the use of language first. Since the language in use must involve the essential patterns of culture including the social structure, value systems, system of knowledge, etc., the study of language can never abandon its social nature. As Mary Douglas states:

> If we ask of any form of communication the simple question what is being communicated? The answer is: information from the social system. The exchange which are being communicated constitute the social system. (qtd. in Halliday, *Language as Social Semiotic: The Social Interpretation of Language and Meaning* 79)

However, SFG concerns more with how social structure determines the various patterns of communication than how a social man cognitively participates in communication. Or it takes rather a sociolinguistic view of semantics than a cognitive view of semantics. It tries to support there is a systematic correspondence between the semiotic structure of the situation type and the functional organization of the semantic system. Each of the main areas of meaning potential tends to be determined or activated by one particular aspect of the situation. (Halliday, *Language as Social Semiotic: The Social Interpretation of Language and Meaning* 116)

We do believe that language users should be regarded as integral whole. As a social man, there is an interaction between language user and language. Language users know how to use language, how to communicate with others, and how to choose appropriate forms of language according to context. But even Halliday himself admits that although the social aspects of language are focused, there is still possibly an intra-organism kind of question. It goes as how the individual can know how to behave in this way. Nevertheless, although Halliday admits the existence of the intra-organism kind of question, he insists that social perspective is more highly significant since a man must be in a certain group and achieve his membership of a group by language. It is language that makes an individual as a person not only a biological specimen of humanity but also a social man. Halliday shows it in a figure as follows (Fig. 3.9):

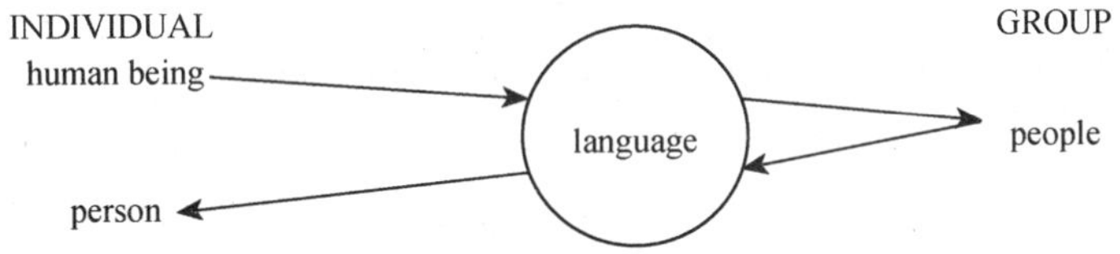

Fig. 3.9 The relation among the individual, the group and language (Ibid. 14)

Generally speaking, the social nature of a man determines the importance of social perspective of language study. Or in Halliday's word, "we explain the nature of the individual as a derivation from and extension of his participation in the group". (Ibid. 14)

But in our opinion, what Halliday reveals about the social nature of an individual can not be a sensible excuse to neglect the intra-organism question. And even the social nature can be a reason for us to emphasize the necessity of combining the two complementary perspectives. The key lies in the question how the individual knows how to behave in this way. Since the nature of an individual is derived and extended from his participation in the group, the formation of an individual's knowledge about how to behave in this way comes mainly from his social experiences. We may well believe that the answer to the intra-organism question must be researched in the social perspective, or it can be a part of language study from the social perspective. According to Peirce's contribution, the concern of cognition can help bring a dynamic and interactive view on language study.

Furthermore, what has been discussed about the "language as social semiotic" generally is under or at most at the level of discourse. It has not been beyond discourse. But linguistic sign process can not only happen within a sign of discourse, but can also among signs. That is to say, any language study at the level of discourse or even within discourse is a kind of micro study. But evidently, language study has to be done beyond micro level, specifically beyond discourse, and focuses on the relationship among discourses, especially as social semiotic. The macro level study of language as social semiotic is about the study of groups of discourse, or sets of discourse, or simply genre. That is the theoretical basis or starting point of what we want to do in our paper. We are to take genre as a kind of macro social semiotic, on the basis of which we try to study the generic intertextuality.

Although Saussure stresses the internal structure of sign system and does not extend the associative and syntagmatic ordering beyond discourse, the idea of non-referentialness and differentialness of language signs may well be applied to the analysis of the relationship among discourses. Furthermore, we follow Peirce's belief that a linguistic sign is identical to a discourse and the interpretant can link signs, which form an endless sign process. And on these bases, we try to combine the inter-organism and the intra-organism or systemic and cognitive and interactive perspective together. In other words, we try to put the intra-organism question within the domain of language study as social semiotic. Or, we are to develop a framework of macro social semiotic by combining the two perspectives.

To explain the idea of genre as macro social semiotic, we are to compare the two key concepts, genre and discourse first, and position them in the system of language respectively.

3.2.2 Discourse or Text

As we have mentioned, greatly influenced by the ideas of context of situation and context of culture as well as the perception of language as speech act, genre is taken to refer to the type of communicative event and often coincide with speech events. (Hymes, *Foundations in Sociolinguistics* 61) And genre carries its own properties such as closely relation with communicative purpose. However, if we compare the definition and properties of genre with those of discourse, the confusion about the difference between genre and discourse is easily aroused.

Before we try to review some efforts on distinguishing between discourse and genre, it is important to note that what we mean in this paper about discourse has little difference with text. As professor Hu Shuzhong argues in the preface of his book *Studies in English Textlinguistics*, text grammar or text linguistics and discourse analysis have been well combined. Although text linguistics and discourse analysis influence different utterances studies respectively, they have a common objective that is to theoretically explain the spoken as well as written language.

Considering some linguists separate the two terms and use them to imply different meanings, we suppose that the achievements of studies in discourse and text can be both applied to our study. The differences between text and discourse held by different linguists are various. According to *The Oxford Companion to the English Language* edited by McArthur, discourse analysis is defined as "in linguistics and semiotics, the analysis of connected speech and writing, and their relationship to the contexts in which they are used. Discourse analysts study written texts, conversation, institutionalized forms of talk, communicative events in general, and aspects of electronic text-processing." (316) And text linguistics is "important in the development of discourse analysis is the work of text grammarians, mostly on written language". (Ibid.) Thus, self-evidently, McArthur takes text as written language and discourse as both spoken and written. But actually this difference has not been well accepted. In *Introduction to Text Lingusitics*, Robert De Beaugrande uses "text" to refer to both spoken utterances and written ones. Or we may well use both text and discourse to refer to both spoken and written utterances.

What's more, the difference between text and discourse can also lie in the belief that text and discourse are two different semiotic structures. Take Basil Hatim for example, text or the set of mutually relevant intentions that serve an overall rhetorical purpose is the ultimate linguistic unit in any activity to do with communicating in language (3), while discourse is about attitudinal and interpersonal component (32). Thus, text and discourse are two items of the basic triad in one model. Text is about compositional plan and texture, and discourse is about attitudinal element. In fact, what Hatim holds is not contradictory with some other linguistic schools' views such as Hallidayean which uses both of two terms interchangeably and do not distinguish them. It is well known that in Systemic Functional Grammar the semantic system of language consists of three functional components including ideational, interpersonal and textual. And only by creating text, language can effectively express ideational and interpersonal meanings. Text is a kind of language in practice. In this sense, Hallidayean text includes the meanings of Hatim's text and his discourse also.

So, we will not distinguish between text and discourse in our paper. But it does not mean that we will take a part of understanding of text or discourse. We tend to imply a comprehensive understanding of discourse or text when we use any one of them in our paper. Discourse or text can refer to both spoken and written utterances, both language action and textual manifestation, both linguistic unit and its attitudinal or interpersonal component, and both the process and the product of an action, etc.

3.2.3 Discourse as Sign in Terms of Semiotics

Different schools have different understandings and definitions of discourse from their own perspectives. For example, the interactional sociolinguistics which stems from anthropology and sociology is concerned with the study of language from the aspect of culture and society. They focus on social interaction through language and study "how people from different cultures may share grammatical knowledge of a language, but differently contextualize what is said — such that very different messages are produced" (Schiffrin 97). They believe that the meanings of natural utterances are determined by circumstances of social life. So they view discourse as a social interaction in which the meaning is facilitated by the use of language.

For Hoey, "text can be defined as the visible evidence of a reasonably self-contained purposeful interaction between one or more writers and one or more readers, in which the writer(s) control the interaction and produce most of (characteristically all) the language". (*Textual Interaction: An Introduction to Written Discourse Analysis* 11)

For Beaugrande, text is a multi-level entity of language, composed of fragments which may or may not be formatted as sentences, since it is an actual system, while sentences are elements of a virtual system. (*Text, Discourse and Process: Toward a Multidisciplinary Science of Texts* 11) So, the text must be defined according to the complete standards of textuality which contains cohesion, coherence, intentionality, acceptability, situationality, intertextuality and informativity rather than a collection of sentences.

Generally speaking, it has been well accepted that discourse is an entity closely connected with action and interaction. Thus the concept of discourse unifies the characteristics of the sign and its contexts which make it capable of conveying action. Discourse is an action-logic with a textual manifestation. (Johansen and Larsen 53)

The well accepted view of discourse supports our assumption that discourse in terms of semiotics should be concerned with both sign system and sign process. Accordingly, it should be taken as a linguistic sign which takes place in three respects. First, the linguistic sign can be located in the whole linguistic sign system or as a whole unit of the system. It can be the sign of other signs and can also be interpreted by other signs. The value of discourse as sign is to be realized by its location in the system as well as its relation with other signs.

Secondly, discourse as sign itself can trigger an endless sign process because of the interpretant. It is a kind of dialogue or interaction, the dialogue between subjects or the interaction with other signs. Probably by the process, certain interconnected roles or positions are established or maintained. The position can be of power where subjects manifest their intentions concerning each other in such a way that those using the signs can change position. (Ibid. 55)

So thirdly, discourse as sign must be relevant with a certain social structure and system, or take place in an institutionalized situation where the interaction and dialogue can be possibly established or maintained. This institutionalized situation serves as the convention we need in the interpretation of discourse as sign.

Conclusively speaking, discourse, in terms of semiotics, is defined as a whole sign which can be located in the corresponding linguistic sign system where it achieves its meaning and value by associative relation and syntagmatic relation, and at the same time as a sign process in which the subjects using it are allocated roles and demarcated where a certain social convention is used or some interaction occurs with other signs by interpretant.

To further support the view of discourse as whole sign, we had better refer to the significance of taking discourse as a whole sign rather than a sign system.

We have discussed a lot about how Halliday develops context from a sociosemantic perspective which involves construing the context of text as a semiotic system manifested in whole or in part through language. This is closely related with Halliday's intrinsic theory of language function since language function is projected onto context as an extrinsic theory of language use. The realization relationship between context and language is treated as a symbolic one, with language a metaphor for social reality at the same time as social reality is a metaphor for language. (Martin, *English Text: System and Structure* 494) As a realization of the social semiotic, the relation between language and its semiotic environment can be shown in Fig. 3.10.

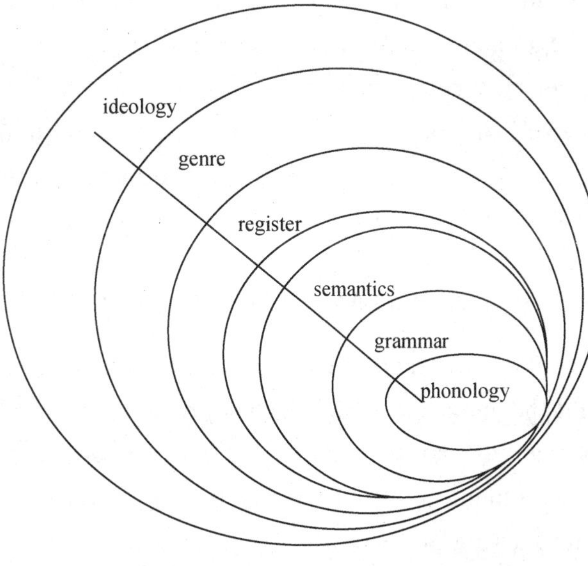

Fig. 3.10 Language and its semiotic environment
(Martin, *English Text: System and Structure* 496)

Based on Hallidayean idea of system, the confusion of difference between genre and discourse seems to be solved. A text is a semantic unit which is not composed of sentences but is realized in sentences. As Halliday says, "a text is to the semantic system what a clause is to the lexicogrammatical system and a syllable to the phonological system". (*Language as Social Semiotic: The Social Interpretation of Language and Meaning* 135) In this sense, text is the configuration of choice from the semantic system. Since the semantic system is organized into functional components, a text as a semantic unit is defined by the textual components. So a text is actually a system of signs but itself is not a sign. Then, genres as types of texts that enact various types of social context are consequently the system of system of sign, each of which "is a staged, goal-oriented social process". (Martin and Rose 7)

So it is evident that Hallidyean idea is greatly influenced and even inherited from Saussure's view of language as system and further develops Saussure's opinion of social semiotic. That is to say, according to Hallidayean idea, when we talk about the system of linguistic sign and the relation between linguistic signs, we have to focus on the discourse level and even under the discourse level, which is what we call as micro study. That is why Halliday emphasizes that being a text must be cohesive and takes register as a complementary part for achieving texture. But in fact, more and more achievements of text linguistics have proven that register or situation context and genre and ideology or sociocultural context share the same importance with cohesion for being a text.

So, we may well say, at the micro-level, these (semiotic semantic) systems of choice form linguistic registers and at the macro-level, discourse genres. (Couture 79) And we are justified to hold a belief that to study language in a more sensible way we have to take a more macro perspective. It is necessary to get a new way to concern the linguistic sign system. We propose that only if we can treat the discourse as a whole sign, we can truly take a macro perspective in language study. In other words, discourse as a whole sign can never be further demarcated into more signs, but is interpreted with triadic components. A word or a sentence can only be meaningful within a discourse. Since Peirce defines anything as a sign depending on whether it is interpreted or not, we argue that discourse as something that can be interpreted meaningful is a whole sign.

3.2.4 Genre as Macro Social Semiosis System

We have mentioned above that we try to combine the language view of sign system and the language view of sign process together. We agree to treat language as a sign system with multi-levels, which can be shown in the model of language and its semiotic environment above. The model with multi-levels indicates to be anthropology-oriented. The starting point of the language study is the relation between language and society. The factor of sociocultural context is considered as a fundamental role in the language theory. According to Martin's explanation about the Halliday's concept of context, it can be further divided into three levels as shown in Fig. 3.11.

According to the figure, Halliday inherits the view of context from Malinowski and Firth and does not divide context into two levels. For him, situation context and cultural context should be at the same level, although he admits that they perform differently. Considering situational context directly provides the concrete settings for discourse while cultural context is "helpful to build in some indication of the cultural background and the assumptions that have to be made if the text is to be interpreted or produced",

(Halliday, *Language, context, and Text: Aspects of Language in a Social-semiotic perspective* 47) Halliday focuses on the situational context but does not offer a separate linguistic model of the context of culture. Halliday defines register as "the configuration of semantic resources that the member of a culture typically associates with a situation type. It is the meaning potential that is accessible in a given social context". (Halliday, *Language as Social Semiotic: The Social Interpretation of Language and Meaning* 111)

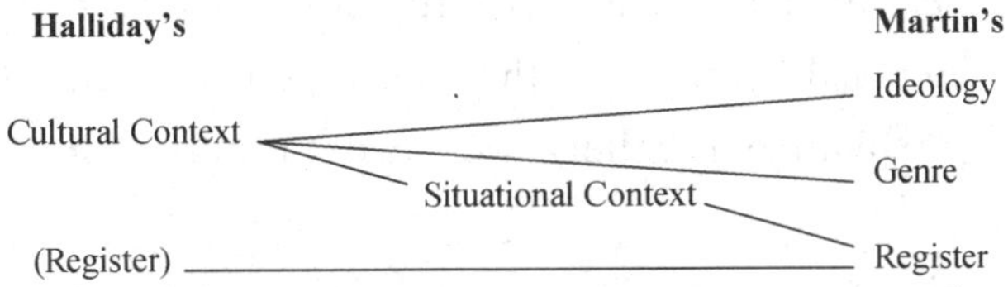

Fig. 3.11 Contrast between Halliday's contextual model and Martin's contextual model (Hu, Zhuanglin and Zhu, Yongsheng 423)

Thus, in this sense, register can be concerned at the same rather than higher level with semantics. However, Martin disagrees on it. In his book of *English Text: System and Structure* Martin, he extends Halliday's use of the term register as context's expression plane to cover additionally part of context's content plane. For Martin, register is used to refer to the semiotic system constituted by the contextual variables field, tenor and mode. (501—502) Obviously, Martin's register is actually Halliday's situational context. In terms of semiotic, register is a semiotic system which can be used to realize the linguistic sign process.

To further cover Halliday's context of culture, Martin proposes a new plane of genre which locates at the higher level of culture. Accordingly, the context of culture is replaced by genre. It is worth to point out that Martin's genre here is different from Halliday' concept of genre. For Halliday, "the various genres of discourse are the specific semiotic functions of text that have social value in the culture. The concept of genre is an aspect of what we are calling the 'mode'". (Halliday, *Language as Social Semiotic: The Social Interpretation of Language and Meaning* 145) But Martin seems greatly influenced by Bakhtin's speech genres and takes genre as "a stage, goal-oriented social process realized through register". (*English Text: System and Structure* 505)

Both Halliday and Martin accept the correlation between genre and socioculture, as "it is the social structure that generates the semiotic tensions and the rhetorical styles and genres that express them". (qtd. in Halliday, *Language as Social Semiotic: The Social Interpretation of Language and Meaning* 79) But Halliday tends to identify register with genre, while Martin formulates genre as a pattern of register patterns so as to "establish genre as a level of semiosis which is not itself metafunctionally organized means that texts can be classified in ways which cut across metafunctional components in langue".

(Martin, *English Text: System and Structure* 505) We prefer Martin's view, since the situational context variables field, tenor and mode can be mostly predictive of semantic choices for a text without referring too much to genre. And even when genre as born with sociocultural factors is used to account for the impossibility of certain combinations of register variables, it takes the role to help interpret.

If we insist on a semiotic view, a problem draws our attention. What is the relation between every two levels in the system? The relation between every two levels in the system has less been discussed by Martin, though he used to mention it as a relation of realization. To better explain our belief, we need to start from Martin's concept of genre.

As we have mentioned above, Martin establishes genre above the register, or according to Martin, genre is a network which manages the relation among register variables. It is genre that organizes the various text types within a network. In this sense, genre can be understood as some criteria that can be applied to interpret the process of combinations of register variables. The reason for Martin failing to make the relation definite probably lies in his original intention of proposing the level of genre that is to explain the schematic structure of discourse. Because of the intention, the role and function of interpretation is missed. But actually, as we have reviewed the achievements from generic studies, genre is decided and functions more than that.

Consequently, we suggest that the nature of relation between two levels in the system should be a kind of sign process. That is to say, discourse is to be processed as a whole sign. And the discourse as a sign is to be the representamen in another semiosis and is interpreted by register with three variables field, tenor and mode. And the combination of register variables as the product of semiosis is to be another representamen in another semiosis and is interpreted by genre. It should be noted that the genre we use here is much more than about schematic structure of discourse. Accordingly, genre should be established as a level of semiosis higher than register, or macro semiosis.

Furthermore, as an abstract concept, genre is actually a system of semiosis in which different sign processes of register interpretation occur. And considering the influence of ideology revealing the closely correlation between language system and social system, we have to assign the social nature to genre. In this sense, genre in semiotic terms can be defined as macro social semiosis system.

What's more, when we define genre as a system of semiosis, we must refer to the concept of modality. We have proven that genre which is born with the sociocultural sense is not only interpreted by socioculture but also participates in the construction of socioculture. Culture is a collective system of socially meaningful practices and correlates with genre. The social practice not only involves language but can also be realized by any practices in the abstract forms of semiosis. It has been well accepted in discourse analysis that discourse is multiply structured. Accordingly, there are various modalities not only language that can be concerned in discourse. So, when the signs of discourses in semiosis of genre are treated in a multi-modal way, there must be other modal genres or action genres realized by other modalities rather than language.

3.2.5 Role of Ideology in Semiotic System

Above the genre, Martine introduces the highest plane of ideology. Generally speaking, Martin defines ideology as the system of coding orientations constituting a culture, which is realized through contextually specific semantic styles associated with groups of speakers of differing generation, gender, ethnicity and class. Ideology is concerned with the redistribution of power — with semiotic evolution. (Ibid. 507) In other words, the plane of ideology seems to evolve the system, mainly showing the unfairness of distribution among the various social communities of semantic potentials. Or it is the tension among discourses that decides the closely correlation between language system and social system. The last plane of ideology is another problem we will try to argue. We hold that the establishment of the four planes of system is not so sensible.

In 2004, on an ideology symposium, Teun A. van Dijk defines the concept of ideology by raising several assumptions of ideology. The first assumption is that, whatever else ideologies are, they are primarily some kind of ideas, that is, belief systems. Hence a cognitive component that is able to properly account for the notion of belief and belief system is needed for a theory of ideology. Secondly, there are no private, personal ideologies. Ideologies are socially shared by the members of a collectivity of social actors. Thus, ideologies consist of social representations that define the social identity of a group, and different types of ideologies are defined by the kind of groups that have an ideology. Thirdly, ideologies as foundational social beliefs of a rather general and abstract nature control and organize other socially shared beliefs. One of the cognitive functions of ideologies is to provide coherence to the beliefs of a group and thus facilitate their acquisition and use in everyday situations. Fourthly, ideologies are relatively stable since they are acquired and changed by many experiences and discourses. Although there can be variability of ideological opinions of group members which should be accounted for at the personal or contextual level, it can not reject the notion of a shared, stable group ideology. Meanwhile, ideologies can also gradually disintegrate.

By the assumptions above, we have got some suggestive conclusions. Firstly, ideologies can influence the whole system as well as the each level of system since they control and organize social shared beliefs which surely guide the distribution of meaning resources. In Martin's own words, "ideology and power run through the whole ensemble of language and culture, positioning people within each social context as having more or less power, and opening or narrowing their access to resources for meaning". (Martin and Rose, *Working with Discourse: Meaning beyond the Clause* 15—16) Secondly, since ideologies as belief systems do not contain societal structure, they can not be used directly to interpret genres. In other words, ideologies are not appropriately established above the level of genre with the relation of realization. Thirdly, there is an interaction between ideologies and discourses. Not only the process of discourse is subjected to ideologies, and ideologies can be acquired and changed by discourses and experiences which can be understood as context. In this sense, we can say there is not only an interaction between ideology and discourse but also an interaction between ideology and genre as well as register.

Based on these conclusions, we argue that ideology should not be established at the level above that of genre as the fourth plane in the system. Ideology should be considered as the monitor in the system. It has many cognitive and social functions at the different levels in the system. Thus, we get our comprehensive system in a macro semiotic approach to text and context with three planes and one monitor as shown in the following Fig. 3.12.

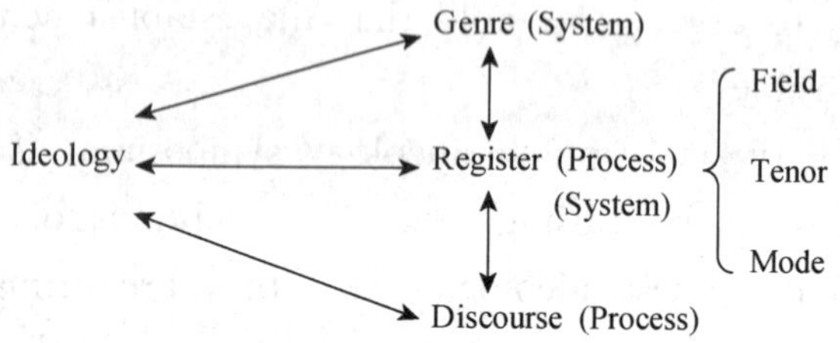

Fig. 3.12 Discourse and its semiotic environment

The figure above shows clearly the position of genre in the system. We argue that genre should be the highest plane in the system. Genre itself is a macro semiosis as well as a semiosis system which involves the semiotic process of register. Register can also serves as a semiosis as well as a sign system with components of field, tenor, mode, and their combinations which play an important role in the sign process of discourse. At the same time, genre is monitored and in turn influences ideology. Generally, the system is a network with each of levels or items mutually connected. Register with three variables corresponding with three functions is the central of the network. It decides the system as the functional correlation of different sign systems. It is worth to emphasize that the system is taken from a macro perspective as we consider discourse as a whole sign and treat it as a sign process. And genre as the highest plane in the system should be concerned as the macro social semiosis system.

3.2.6 Summary

What we talk about the position and role in the system of language and its semiotic environment helps us a lot to study generic intertextuality identity.

Our rationale construction partly comes from Saussure as well as his followers and partly from Peirce's approach. According to Peirce, language is a kind of symbolic sign system which is characterized by being arbitrary. That is to say, symbolic signs are built up or used as signs for given purposes or conventional designations with a certain meaning because of conventional usage. Moreover, the conventions used in linguistic symbolic sign process are the generalized social conventions rather than private. This view is agreed by Saussure, although he never uses the word of symbol in the way.

And Saussure even further stresses the systematic relationship between linguistic signs, since the symbolic sign must be supported by a clear differentiation between the symbolic signs themselves. As he states,

> in language there are only differences. Even more important: a difference generally implies positive terms between which the difference is set up; but in language there are only differences without positive terms. Whether we take the signified or the signifier, language has neither ideas nor sounds that existed before the linguistic system, but only conceptual and phonic differences that have issued from the system. (qtd. in Johansen and Larsen 46)

Obviously, in Saussure's opinion, "language — which is collective and governed by internalized rules used well-nigh unconsciously — is in several important ways built just like a purposely planned system". (Ibid. 48) It is also well accepted by many structuralist linguists that a sign's meaning content can be analyzed like its expression and can be divided into non-signs, content figure. But considering what we have argued in our model of language system above, when Saussure focuses on the word or even the sound pattern as a sign unit we take discourse as a whole sign and register as well as genre as a semiotic system. Thus, the study of genre has nothing to do with a whole sign analysis.

3.3 A Three-Dimensional Framework of Generic Intertextuality

In this section, we try to apply partly Peirce's approach and the views of Saussure as well as his followers such as Halliday to the study in generic intertextuality. Specifically speaking, we will borrow Saussure's distinction between system and process and apply it to our study in generic intertextuality, hence extending it to a higher level of application.

It is worth to note that what we mean by system is not to accept Saussure's radical idea of the materiality of linguistic signs or what Saussure emphasizes on the value of a sign lying in its relation to other signs. What we imply by system is a kind of resources rather than structure which can be chosen from a network of potentials. And to fulfill a comprehensive research with multi-perspectives concerned, the cognitive and the newly understood sociocultural and interactive approach will also be involved. Accordingly, we partly follow the Peirce's emphasis on semiosis as a process and his view of interaction and interpretation. Actually, it is Peirce's idea of dialogical thought that leads us to take the perspective of intertextuality to study genre. Or since the nature of genre is intertextual, it is necessary and possible to study generic intertextuality.

As we have discussed in 3.2.1.2, Peirce's emphasis on semiosis as a process produces the thought of dialogue which is further developed in the theories of Bakhin, and his view of interaction and interpretation essentially represents the idea of intertextuality. Pierce argues that "all thinking is dialogic in form. You self of one instant appeals to your deeper self for his assent". (qtd. in Chandler 34) Since anyone who lives in a certain society must carry the traits of society and one's view of anything develops from his or her experiences as well as other discourses, we can understand the dialogue between you self and your deeper self as the interaction between this sign process and other interpretations from other sign processes. The same case is to be with genre as a semiosis system with symbolic signs within it. That is why we claim that genre in nature is of generic intertextuality. The generic intertextuality is in essence the relation of components within the semiosis system of genre. In this sense, generic intertextuality is a kind of system of resources, and underlies a dynamic process with interaction and cognition. Conclusively, generic intertextuality involving the interactive relation among semiotic processes of genre should be viewed in terms of semiotic systems of signification with ideology monitoring to offer an account of how particular combinations of register variables are cultural-specific.

Traditionally, there are three fields in the semiotic studies. They are the study on semiotic itself with focus on its content or types or ways to deliver meanings, the study on the semiotic process including information passing, semiotic production and interpretation, and the study on culture in which semiotic is used. (Hu Zhuanglin, "Multimodalization in Social Semiotics" 5) Since we try to construct a comprehensive theoretical framework of generic intertextuality, we are expected to cover all of them. If what we discuss about generic intertextuality system is the first type of study, what we will concern after the system should be about the second and third types.

So, we propose the second perspective to discuss generic intertextuality, generic intertextuality process. We emphasize a lot the interaction and cognition of generic intertextuality. Then what is its mechanism? Or how can a subject know what to choose from the resources and how to reorganize the information from the potentials to realize the process of generic intertextuality. And we even should concern the motivation of a particular process, that is, to answer why a subject chooses so, which had to be put in the culture and social representation or ideology. The motivation is discussed in generic intertextuality focus as the third dimension in our study in generic intertextuality.

3.3.1 Generic Intertextuality System

The view of language as system with the systematic relationship between linguistic signs not only holds true for basic elements but also for larger differences of meaning. (Johansen and Larsen 49) As we have discussed, genre is the highest plane in the language system which itself is a semiosis system. Thus, we may well try to apply the idea of differentiation into the system of genre.

Although we have some doubts about many structuralist linguists' well accepted view that a sign's meaning content can be analyzed like its expression and can be divided into non-signs, content figure, it does not matter for our application of this view of system a lot since according to our model genre itself is treated as a semiosis system taking social actions as signs. Thus, the content figures or components in the system do not involve the matter. They can be signs which should be explained in other signs that function as their interpretants.

As we have mentioned above, generic intertextuality involving the interactive relation among semiotic processes of genre should be viewed in terms of semiotic systems of signification. It must be pointed out that this kind of interactive relations are dynamic with semiotic processes of genre being unlimited. According to our model of discourse and its context environments, genre is the knot in the system which links register and ideology directly. In this way, each semiotic process of genre is a result of choices from the semiotic system of genre in which the generic components can be used as interpretant to semiosis of register variables and meanwhile be interpreted in a semiotic process of genre. Thus, generic intertextuality can be assumed as a semiosis system of resources in which the interactive relations with field, tenor and mode which respectively corresponds with ideational function, interpersonal function and textual function are realized. And all of these are monitored by ideology.

Since we use semiosis to refer to the semiotic entity within the system, we take the view of interpretation on semiotic process. In Peirce's terms, interpretant is the key to make any sign to be sign with meanings being produced. The interpretation itself is dynamic because it involves a subject. It is the subject that realizes the signification of semiotic system by choosing from resources. As a matter of fact, there is also an interaction between resources and subject. Or the objective resources are internalized or cognized by subjects. Thus, taking the subject into account, we propose that potentials of generic itertextuality system involve the disciplinary knowledge potentials and macro speech-act potentials, evaluation potentials, and modality potentials. Each set of potentials stems from its own categories. Specifically speaking, the knowledge potentials are of conceptual category, the macro speech-act potentials are of structural category, the evaluation potentials are of ideological category and the modality potentials are of formal category.

3.3.2 Generic Intertextuality Process

We take the dimension of generic intertextuality process to answer the question as how a subject can know what to choose from the resources and how to reorganize the information from the potentials to realize the process of generic intertextuality.

We assume at the very beginning that meanings are not carried but interpreted, as Mark Turner put it:

> Expressions do not mean; they are prompts for us to construct meanings by working with processes we already know. In no sense is the meaning of [an] ... utterance "right there in the words." When we understand an utterance, we in no sense are understanding "just what the words say"; the words themselves say nothing independent of the richly detailed knowledge and powerful cognitive processes we bring to bear. (qtd. in Fauconnier, *Mental Spaces: Aspects of Meaning Construction in Natural Language* XXII)

Taking genre as macro social semiotic in partly Peirce's approach, we think generic intertextuality must involve cognition and interaction between subject and sociocultural context. And to answer the question as how a subject can know what to choose from the resources and how to reorganize the information from the potentials to realize the process of generic intertextuality is about the mechanism of realization of generic intertextuality or the process of generic intertextuality.

We have got totally four sets of potentials as components of the semiosis system of generic intertextuality. The conclusion of these potentials stems from our analysis on register variables as well as their application in a certain socioculture with a certain ideology by subject. That is to say, contexts involving these potentials are to be treated as cognitive representations.

According to cognitive linguistics, we can use cognitive models to cover all the stored cognitive representations that belong to a certain field. Specifically speaking, cognitive models can have at least four perspectives, frame, schema, script and plan. We argue that the four sets of potentials in generic intertextuality system take different cognitive models respectively to process. For example, knowledge can be viewed as an array in which elements are arranged such that access of potentially relevant elements is provided. (Beaugrande, *Text*, *Discourse and Process: Toward a Multidisciplinary Science of Texts* 163) This is called a frame. To reach the goal of a macro speech act, we need a schema to guide what to occur during actualization and a plan to help advance. Some instructions to participants about what should be said and what should be done in their respective roles need a script. In this sense, the four potentials can be represented by their respective cognitive models. And since cognitive models are the configurations of mental spaces or structures of mental spaces, we can get the mental space of genre as macro social semiosis by the roles defined by models as well as the values for those roles which represent the conceptual structures in potentials. Thus, generic intertextuality process is actually the process of blending and integration of genre spaces which are constructed by models representing the conceptual structures in the potentials of generic intertextuality system.

3.3.3 Generic Intertextuality Focus

The discussion of generic intertextuality process above shows us a sensible way to understand the cognitive mechanism of generic intertextuality by applying the conceptual integration theory or blending space theory which is originated proposed by Fauconnier.

It is emphasized that conceptual integration occurs as an on-line and dynamic cognitive construction whose central process is conceptual blending. Fauconnier and Turner use many examples to illustrate the central principles of the network model of conceptual integration for local purpose of thought and action. According to their researches, there are four mental spaces participating the blending. They are input spaces, generic space and blended space by which some necessary conditions for blending are satisfied.

According to Fauconnier, the necessary conditions used in the blending are cross-space mapping, generic space, blend and emergent structure. Briefly speaking, cross-space mapping means part of elements in the input spaces must be mapped. Generic space is a kind of operation space to indicate the shared abstract structures or points by mapping input spaces. Blend implies input spaces being partly projected into the fourth space of blended space. And emergent structure is to show the complexity of the blending process. Three principles are used in the process including composition, completion and elaboration.

In the application of blending theory to the generic intertextuality process, the input spaces of genres are mapped by the generic space into the blended space with the emergent structure. So, if our discussion of generic intertextuality process is about how convincing and powerful the blending theory is in revealing the cognitive mechanism of generic intertextuality, the third dimension of our generic intertextuality is to answer why this part of input spaces is mapped, not the others, or to answer why a subject chooses so, which had to be put in the culture and social representation or ideology, or how the space blending can happen or what is the motivation of the blending.

Generally speaking, we try to prove that the process of generic intertextuality is ultimately determined by the function of a user's intention. A user conventionally focuses only on specific components from a whole set of resources. Thus, only this but not that part of input spaces is mapped.

In a more global perspective of genre as macro social semiosis system, we will further try to explore the role of ideology functioning on the focus. And by doing so, we try to prove that there is always an interaction between ideology and generic intertextuality. They are mutually influenced and interdependent.

Chapter Four

Generic Intertextuality System

We have constructed a three-dimensional theoretical model for generic intertextuality study with a macro social semiotic rationale. In this chapter, we will focus on the first dimension of generic intertextuality study. In the dimension of generic intertextuality system, generic intertextuality is a resource system with sets of potentials, including disciplinary potentials, macro-speech act potentials, evaluation potentials, and modality potentials. With the help of genre studies, we will discuss disciplinary potentials, macro-speech act potentials and evaluation potentials; while by referring to studies on multimodalities in semiotics we will bring about modality potentials. We hope to give a relatively comprehensive view of generic intertextuality system in the form of potential.

4.1 Disciplinary Knowledge Potentials

4.1.1 Knowledge and Disciplinary Knowledge

In the different domains, the notion of knowledge is defined differently. For example, the philosophical enquiry focuses on fundamental issues of the nature of knowledge, and traditionally defines it as justified true beliefs. And psychology and Artificial Intelligence defines it as mental representations in memory which provides a conceptual framework for interacting with the world. Although linguistics has traditionally ignored the role of knowledge, the late Paul Werth made interesting proposals on the role of knowledge in discourse. His most outstanding contribution on knowledge probably lies in his study in the role of shared knowledge in communication and his further division of knowledge into general knowledge and mutual knowledge. His achievements can be shown in Fig. 4.1.

Thus, the traditional definition of knowledge is all from the cognitive perspective. But later, some linguists add more into the understanding of knowledge, such as Foucault and van Dijk. For most of them, knowledge is constructed by a set of statements, hence born with the power of social institutions. Thus, knowledge is not only mental, but also social, as van Dijk states:

> Knowledge is acquired, shared and used by people in interaction, as well as by groups, institutions and organizations. Indeed, without such a social basis, knowledge would be no more than personal belief. Consensus, common sense or common ground are among the many notions that define this social dimension of knowledge. (van Dijk, "The Discourse-Knowledge Interface" 86)

The assumption of the application of knowledge to the linguistic studies especially the text linguistics is based on the belief that all kinds of knowledge are achieved by description and organized in discourses by media. The relation between world and us is actually the relation between discourses. Anything that deviates from discourse does not exist. (qtd. in Qian Minru 83) Shared knowledge is shown in Fig. 4.1.

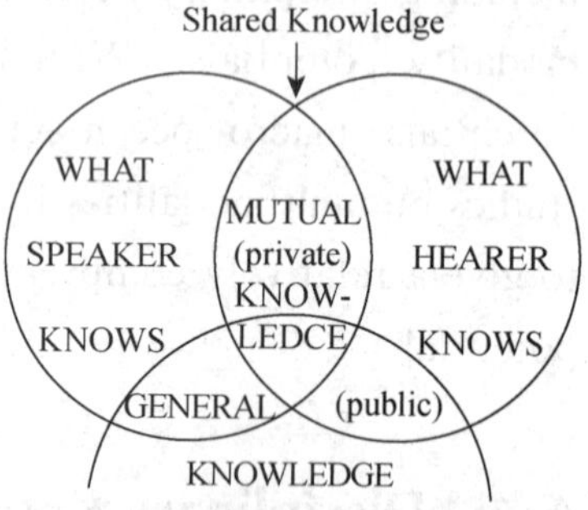

Fig. 4.1 Shared knowledge (Werth 94)

Based on the studies of knowledge in general, we come to disciplinary knowledge which is defined by *The New Oxford Dictionary of English* as a branch of knowledge. According to Paul Werth in his *Text Worlds: Representing Conceptual Space in Discourse*, general, or public, knowledge consists of all that information which is in principle available to all individuals by virtue of their membership in various larger social groupings. (96) Accordingly, we may well understand disciplinary knowledge as information which is available to an individual by virtue of his membership in a particular disciplinary field or discipline.

Disciplines in the world take different subjects as their own targets of studies and are also delimitated by them. As a branch of knowledge, no discipline can be realized without language. And furthermore, under different backgrounds of sociocultures, different disciplines are socially defined and accepted. The change and emergence of old and new disciplines occur with the development of society within a certain culture. In this sense, disciplines must be mapped and reflected by genres which have been taken as social events. If we take a more closely look at it, it could be proven by the register variable of field which is monitored by socioculture and ideology. In other words, the register variable of field can correspond with discipline in genre studies.

The development of society brings along the development of disciplines. On the one hand, disciplines are being more and more specific and profession-oriented. On the other hand, more and more multi-disciplinary events are emerging. Both of them support the necessity and inevitability of generic intertextuality. As a matter of fact, disciplinary knowledge provides a resource for generic intertextuality, representing as disciplinary knowledge potentials of generic intertextuality.

4.1.2 Elements in Disciplinary Knowledge Potentials

4.1.2.1 Theme of Discipline

Each discipline must have a subject as its target of study. This is what we call as the theme of discipline. Take the discipline of economy for example, economics is "the science of the production and distribution of wealth as well as the application of this to a particular subject". Or briefly speaking, discipline of economy is the knowledge about the "wealth and resources of a community, esp. in terms of the production and consumption of goods and services", according to the definition of economy in *The Concise Oxford Dictionary*.

If a genre is mostly about the theme of a certain discipline, we will naturally take it as a certain disciplinary genre, such as economic genre, legal genre and medical genre, etc. Some studies on genre analysis under the sociolinguistic approach are the best proofs of it. Bhatia, for instance, indicates the distinguishable legal genre can depend on "the background knowledge that such participants bring in the situation in which that particular event is embedded and a number of other factors". (*Analysing Genre: Language Use in Professional Settings* 101) It is sensible to understand the background knowledge to be the professional knowledge as the discourse community is highlighted in such studies as ESP.

4.1.2.2 Discourse Community of Discipline

According to Swales, established members of discourse communities employ genres to realize communicatively the goal of their communities. (*Genre Analysis: English in Academic and research settings* 52) The recognition of genre within a discipline partly depends on the disciplinary knowledge which not only encompasses the theme of the discipline, but also the organization of the theme of the discipline. As Jones' research on medical consultations shows that the established members of the discourse community of medicine, specifically medical doctors, are trained to use the system of SOAP to structure their consultations. SOAP specifically means:

S = Subjective (what the patient says is wrong; what the patient perceives as his or her symptoms);

O = Objective (result of tests; symptoms perceived by the doctor);

A = Analysis (of the symptoms so as to lead to a diagnosis);

P = Prescription (Pharmaceutical and / or giving advice or treatment).
(Ibid. 54)

However, when patients complain and get advices from doctors, they are rarely aware of the order doctors impose on the consultation by using a structuring system. It is medical doctors who manage the consultation and guide patients to follow, since "active discourse community members tend to have the greatest genre-specific expertise". (Ibid. 54—55)

Not all talks about one's illness between a man who is ill and a man whose profession is medicine can be taken as medical consultation. Only if the medical doctor activates the knowledge of consultation and uses it to process the talk, the talk can be defined as a medical consultation. The underlying logic or rationale the established members of a discourse community have is facilitative in both reception and production of a genre. As Erickson and Schultz observe in their study on academic counseling sessions, "there is a similar sequential order of discourse topics across interviews — an order which manifests an underlying logic of gatekeeping decision making". (12) It is the knowledge shared by the established members of a discourse community that decides the underlying logic or the interactional deep structure. In this sense, the underlying logic or the interactional deep structure reflects the particular way of information processing in a certain discipline. Probably, there is a most suitable research approach to a certain discipline.

The role of discourse community is also illustrated by the subdivision of a discipline which is adopted and used by professionals. Hence, more and more new genres within a certain discipline are created and widely accepted. For example, under the broadest genre of legal discipline, there are lawyer-client consultation, counsel-witness examination in spoken form and legislation, contracts, agreements etc. in written form used in various professional settings. (Bhatia, *Analysing Genre: Language Use in Professional Settings* 101) These subgenres within the domain of legal discipline can only be created and first used by the professionals who are mostly involved in those subgenres. So, the knowledge within a discipline that decides genre is a distinctive package of social identities manifested communicatively.

4.1.2.3 Process of Discipline

Although we admit the important and incontestable position of underlying logic or interactional deep structure in decision of genre within a domain of discipline, we have to realize that "it is not the underlying logic, the interactional deep structure, that is essential, for much more is manifested in performance — in communicational surface structure — than an underlying abstract logic". (Ibid.) The underlying abstract logic here is embedded in the process of discipline.

As to the process of discipline, there is a convincing result of the experiment done by Johns and Dudley-Evans in 1980. A subject-specific English class for the Development Administration Group is set up to concentrate on reading skills in the first term and on the training of writing skills in the second term. The selected texts in the training cover a wide range of subjects in the fields of administration, economics, finance, politics and sociology written by authors with a wide range of academic backgrounds. After two terms of training, the result shows that the difficulty for most students in the subject-specific English class does not lie in the fact that a large number of unfamiliar technical terms, but that the students find it difficult to perceive the conceptual framework, or more specifically, the taxonomic system underlying those technical terms. (qtd. in Johns, "The Text and its Message" 107) It can be inferred from the experiment that for the expert members of a discourse community in their professional domain there is an underlying abstract logic decided by the discipline.

Another most well-known achievement to illustrate the process of discipline is probably van Dijk's study on the super-structure. In his *News as Discourse*, van Dijk points out that

> the overall meaning (macrostructure) of discourse has more than its own organizing principles. It also needs some kind of overall syntax, which defines the possible forms in which topics or themes can be inserted and ordered in the actual text. [...] This global form of discourse can be defined in terms of a rule-based schema. Such a schema consists of a series of hierarchically ordered categories, which may be specific for different discourse types and conventionalized and hence different in various societies or cultures. (49)

Van Dijk further indicates that many discourse types in our culture have more-or-less fixed schematic organizations. But the schemata used in professional domains require special training for the professional discourse community users. For example, scientific discourse may have a conventional form which often features an argumentative schema that a number of "Premises" are followed by a "Conclusion"; psychological articles may even have a fixed, normative form which requires an "Introduction" or "Theory Section", an "Experimental section" that itself has subcategories such as "Design" "Materials" "Subjects", and a final "Discussion section". (Ibid.)

The schema here is comprised of categories which associate the macro propositions in the macro structure with concrete discursive functions. The schema leads us to believe that a disciplinary genre must be realized with its particular underlying logic or interactional deep structure performed by surface structure. In other words, any discipline has its own way to process so that its corresponding disciplinary genre is born with an established overall structure created and adopted and spread by the established members of the discourse community within the domain of discipline.

Take the genre of legal provision for example, several theoretically possible categories are established. They are the category of form taken in the legal settings to indicate clearly whether it is legislation, decree or regulation, the category of name of institution who is the responsible authority to draft the legal provision, the category of title to show the general content, the category of foreword to show the purposes and tasks of the legal provision, the category of body in the form of volume, chapter, section, item, and article sequentially, the category of claim to abolish other relevant legislation, the category of time to take effect, and the category of signature. (Qian, Minru 114—115) It has to be noted that not all the theoretically possible categories must be contained in the configuration of a genre but only some of them will be chosen to perform.

4.1.3 Summary

As we have mentioned above, the development of society brings along the development of disciplines in two ways, one of which is more and more multi-disciplinary events are emerging. Because of the combination of disciplines, new disciplines are developed. Hence new corresponding genres are created. In terms of discipline, new disciplinary genres are born with the traces of multi-disciplines involved by integrating some of their disciplinary knowledge. They can be the theme of discipline, the underlying logic or the interactional deep structure processed by the discourse community of discipline, the performing schema closely related with semantic macro structure. All of them are of disciplinary knowledge. In this sense, we conclude that the generic intertextuality can be realized by disciplinary knowledge. By referring to other disciplinary knowledge, we can combine and integrate other disciplinary genres.

4.2 Macro-Speech Act Potentials

4.2.1 Macro-Structure

It has been well proven by van Dijk that a semantic characterization of discourse structures should also be given on a level of a more global organization, that of macro-structures. (van Dijk, *Text and Context: Explorations in the Semantics and Pragmatics of Discourse* 130) Macro-structures are characterized in terms of proposition. Roughly speaking, propositions are the smallest, independent meaning constructs of language and thought. (van Dijk, *News as Discourse* 31) Or propositions are the smallest semantic units. Macro-structures are organized with sets of propositions. These propositions are not directly expressed but indirectly implied within large stretches of text. To differentiate this kind of propositions from others that expressed by clauses or sentences, these propositions are given distinguishing titles as "macro-propositions".

From a more concrete point of view, the notion of macro-structure is to be approached by the explication of discourse topic, which seems to reduce, organize and categorize semantic information of sequences as wholes. In other words, a conceptual structure of (macro) propositions can be a discourse topic if it hierarchically organizes the conceptual (propositional) structure of the sequence. (van Dijk, *Text and Context: Explorations in the Semantics and Pragmatics of Discourse* 134) Furthermore, given a large stretch of text can include several topics or themes, macro-structures can be organized with a set of macro-propositions.

Van Dijk studies much about the macro-structure of news and finds the particular features of macro-structure of news discourse. Take the news item printed in the overseas section about East Timor under the heading "East Timor's plight" for example:

East Timor's plight

Shultz joins critics of Indonesian rule

From Our Correspondent, Jakarta

Mr. George Shultz, the US Secretary of State, yesterday unexpectedly raised the issue of congressional concern over continuing Indonesian military activity in East Timor in a meeting with the Foreign Minister Professor Mochtar Kusumaatmadja.

Mr. Shultz, who is here to attend an expanded Asean (Association of South East Asian Nations) foreign ministers' meeting, carried with him a letter of concern signed by a bipartisan group of 123 congressmen. The letter said that the plight of East Timor, annexed by Indonesia after bloody fighting in the middle and late 1970s, was very much the concern of the United States as long as America continued to supply arms used in the territory.

The letter urged Jakarta to give unrestricted access to relief and humanitarian organizations, journalists and independent observers, and expressed concern over reports of the situation worsening since the Indonesian Army launched a new operation — still continuing — in the area last August.

Much of the source material used by the Congressmen came from the East Timorese apostolic delegate, Mr. Carlos Felipe Belo, who said in a letter that about 100,000 of an estimated 600,000 people in East Timor had died since the conflict began.

Diplomatic sources pointed out that Mr. Shultz has raised the subject with Professor Kusumaatmadja on the same day the ruling Labor Party in neighboring Australia passed a strongly worded resolution. This was considered a narrow victory for the moderate faction in Australian Government in that it did not call for self-determination for East Timor.

The text of the Canberra resolution, however, expressed grave concern in remarkably similar terms over the renewed fighting.

The Australian press and left wing of the Labor Party have been the most vocal critics of Indonesian policy in East Timor, while the United States has expressed its regret over the lack of an act of self-determination, while accepting Indonesian sovereignty. ①

Van Dijk assigns a macro-proposition to each paragraph at the first level of macro-structure and further gives a figure to show the organization of the Shultz and East Timor item. The figure of the thematic structure of the news report is shown in Fig. 4.2.

The macro-proposition for each paragraph:

1. Shultz, U. S. Secretary of State, raised the issue of congressional concern about Indonesian military actions in East Timor, during a meeting with Foreign Minister Mochtar Kusumaatmadja.
2. Shultz carried a letter from members of Congress, saying that the plight of East Timor was of concern to the United States.
3. The letter urged free access to the area by independent organizations of the Indonesia army.
4. The letter used materials from the East Timorese apostolic delegate about the death of many people.
5. Shultz's declaration coincided with an Australian Labor Party resolution.
6. The resolution expressed grave concern about the new fighting in East Timor.
7. The Australian left and the press were the most vocal critics of Indonesian policy, whereas the United States regrets lack of self-determination while accepting Indonesian sovereignty.

In the thematic respect, it is obvious that the protests of Shultz are conditioned by the letter from members of the U. S. Congress. And the letter again is the condition of new information about victims in East Timor. Thus, this typical news discourse can

① The news item was printed in the overseas section in *Times* 12 Jul. 1984, qtd. in van Dijk, *News As Discourse* (Hillsdale NJ: Lawrence Erlbaum Associates, Inc., 1988)

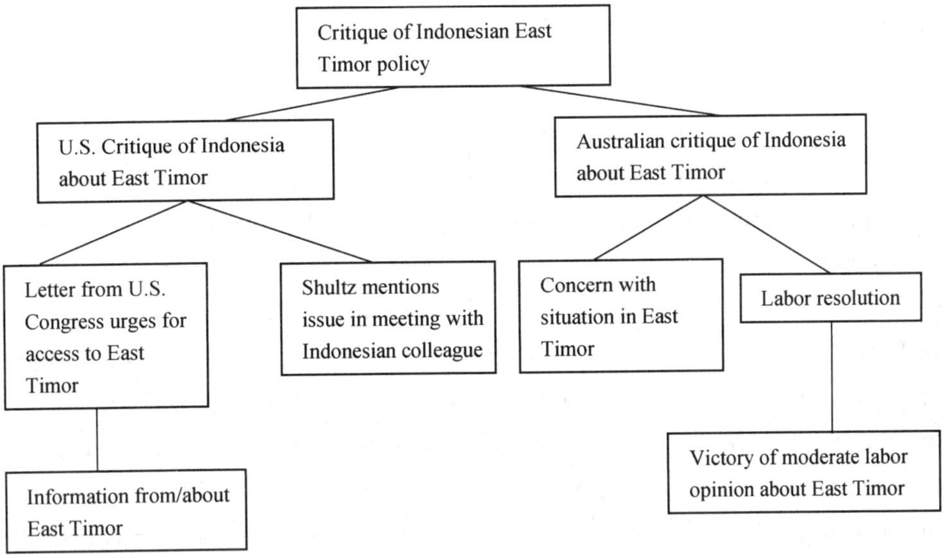

Fig. 4. 2 Representation of the simplified thematic structure of the news report about Shultz/East Timor (Ibid. 42)

represent that condition or cause and consequence relation seems to be the important organizing feature of thematic structure. Another outstanding and typical feature of topic realization in news discourse is its installment. That is to say, each topic is only represented in its part, not as a whole. It may be caused by the top-down principle of relevance organized in news.

Thus, from his analysis, van Dijk concluded:

> news discourse may exhibit a thematic realization structure that is basically (1) top-down; (2) relevance controlled; and (3) cyclical (in installments). That is, main acts and participants that are politically relevant come first, followed in each cycle by details of main participants, identity of secondary participants, components/conditions/consequences/manner of acts, time and location details, etc. Political relevance as a criterion for thematic realization means that those conditions or consequences and participants are mentioned first that are compatible with the newspaper's and readers' model of the situation in general, and of the recent events in particular. (*News as Discourse* 48)

Macro-structure is the universal principle of semantic structure for any discourse of natural language. But obviously in different domains, it may be unfolded with various typical features involving its cognitive operations.

4.2.2 Macro-Rules

The whole macro-structure has a hierarchical organization in which each sequence of macro-propositions can be subsumed under a higher level macro-proposition. (van Dijk, *News as Discourse* 32) Then it seems necessary to make the use of macro-rules to link the lower level propositions with higher level propositions. In some sense, macro-rules are semantic mapping rules or transformations. It can be concluded that topics or themes are derived from the meanings of a text by such macro-rules. Topics in the news may be organized, realized, expressed, or signaled in a specific way. That is to say, there should be special macro-rules to which the organization of themes should conform.

Considering "one of the cognitive functions of macro-structures is the organization, in processing and memory, of complex semantic information", and "language users can not, and need not, store all the propositional information of a given discourse in verbal processing", (van Dijk, *Text and Context: Explorations in the Semantics and Pragmatics of Discourse* 143) the macro-rules used to get macro-structure are actually the operation rules of semantic information reduction. Accordingly, van Dijk proposes totally four macro-rules. The first rule of information reduction is deletion, by which accidental information is to be deleted. The second rule is also a kind of deletion rule operating under different conditions, where the deleted information is not accidental but constitutional of a certain concept or frame. The third operation is that of simple generation. And the last operation is another form of generation which involves essential information and the deleted information denotes essential properties, causes, components, consequences, etc of higher level facts.

However, later van Dijk seems to modify the macro-rules. According to his views in *News as Discourse*, the macro-rules of information reduction are deletion, construction and generalization. By the macro-rule of deletion, information is very simply left out. For example, "a little town" can be shown in the logical representation as town(a) & little(a) → town(a) with the schema of $f(x) \,\&\, g(x) \rightarrow f(x)$. The deleted information of $g(x)$ in the formula must be a sort of accidental information. This sort of information usually serves as an attributive or detailed predicate rather than an identifying or conceptual predicate, which can be left out without changing or influencing the interpretation of other information. The second rule is generalization. In contrast with the rule of deletion, the information left out by this rule is not accidental or even sometimes not detailed, but rather essential. A more inherent property is abstracted so as to generalize the specific information. The schema for this operation is: $< f(x) \,\&\, g(x) > \rightarrow h(x)$; Condition: $(f(x) \rightarrow h(x)) \,\&\, (g(x) \rightarrow h(x))$. By this operation, we can generalize a cat, a dog, a bird into a pet, if we refer to the properties of the superordinate class of pet. We can get "there were toys lying around" to express a macro-proposition for a sequence like "there was a ball, a doll, a toy-car lying around". The last rule is construction. It is also a kind of generalization and also involves essential information. The information left out is not deleted but combined and integrated according to a more general concept or frame of an event, as it usually denotes causes, components, and consequences of the event. Thus, the sequence of "I bought wood, stones and concrete; I laid foundations; I erected walls, I made a roof, etc." can be constructed into "I built a house". The schema for the operation can be shown as: $< f(x) \ \& \ g(x) > \rightarrow h(x)$; Condition: $h(x) \rightarrow < f(x) \ \& \ g(x) >$.

4.2.3 Macro-Action and Macro-Speech Act

Macro-structure and macro-rules are theoretically taken as the universal principles of semantic structure and semantic information reduction for any discourse of natural language. However, as van Dijk points out, "due to various cognitive factors, the actually constructed cognitive macro-structures may be different for different language users, or different for the same language user in different pragmatic contexts or social situations". (van Dijk, *Text and Context: Explorations in the Semantics and Pragmatics of Discourse* 147) Once the factors of context or social situation are involved, the focus of language research turns to the speech act or the pragmatic discourse that contains structure of text and context.

If discourse is treated semantically as the unit of (macro) propositions, discourse can be represented in a macro way by macro-structure which is realized by macro-rules. But if we take discourse as a speech act, discourse is only an individual speech act. That is to say, treating discourse as an individual speech act is the study of natural language in a micro way rather than a macro way. Thus, it seems necessary to come to a global, overall structure of communicative interaction, which involves a sequences of speech acts but not individual speech act.

It must be pointed out that a discourse as a speech act is an integral whole of complex actions or a macro-action. When we identify discourse with macro-action, it seems necessary to make clear the notion of action. The notion of action is usually treated in close connection with that of event, as the definition of action shows that an action is an event brought about by a human being.

To understand the notion of action, we can refer to the notion of event first. One basic concept involved in the definition of the notion of event is "change" which implies a difference between world-states or situations and hence requires a temporal ordering of worlds. If we try to divide time into abstract units described as previous or subsequent in the linear sequence of time, event means a change along with the states or a set of possible worlds. When we open the door, we change the state of the previous state of the door being closed. So the event of opening the door occurs. In brief, once the state of a possible world changes from the initial state to the final state, an event occurs. And events can be defined according to change, which are accomplished by act representing in language as predicate.

Although an event may be assigned properties, we still have one predicate for the event as one distinct event to unify the infinite series of intermediary phases of the event, because only the initial state / final state difference is relevant for our actions and interactions. For example, the door may be opened widely, opened slowly and opened with loud sound or not, identifying the different states in the continuous time of the event. But none of them will be involved in the identification of the event of opening the door. The basic concept of the notion of event proves that event is itself a compound event which is constituted by several events. These events are linearly ordered but perceived or conceived of as one event at a certain level of description. The component events may in other situations occur or as components in other compound events. (van Dijk, *Text and Context: Exploration in the Semantics and Pragmatics of Discourse* 168—169) In this case, the component events should be identical with the specific speech acts, while the compound event is identical with the macro-action.

It is on this basis that we can talk about the rules we use to get the macro-speech act from a series of speech acts. As to how we can get the macro-speech act from a series of speech acts, we can refer to the macro-rules as we use in the process of semantic information by semantic macro-structure. It is assumed that actions, just like semantic information, are organized in higher level units and structures. More specifically, sequences of doings are assigned hierarchical action structures, planned and interpreted as such, at various level of macro-organization. (Ibid. 233) Van Dijk gives a concrete example: when I want to go to Paris, a certain number of actions may be involved. The most global action is that I am going to Paris. This is the macro-action that determines several specific actions such as going to visit my aunt, by train, and next week.

So, the macro-action can be interpreted by the lower level sequences of specific actions. And at the same time, the macro-action can activate the action frame of lower levels so as to form a hierarchical structure with various levels and even the relevant actions at each level. For example, "going or traveling to Paris" will activate the train or journey action frame, containing "reserving seats" "buying tickets" "going to the railway station", etc. as preparatory actions, "getting into the carriage" "choosing a seat" "disposing of luggage" "reading a newspaper" or "talking with co-passengers", as obligatory or optional component actions.

Generally speaking, discourse as a way to communicate is a complex action with a series of specific speech acts arranged into a hierarchical structure. According to the Speech Act Theory proposed by Austin in *How to Do Things with Words*, there are three kinds of acts for a speech act, locutionary act, illocutionary act, and perlocutionary act. Some studies on the relationship between illocutionary act and type of speech act indicate that the surface link or sequential structure of component events within a discourse as a compound event can not be the foundation to describe discourse. It is the hierarchical structure of illocutionary acts that serve as the basis to describe discourse as compound event. (Qian, Minru 48)

In this sense, the key to define a macro-speech act can not possibly depend on its component events, but on the functions of such events in interaction. The hierarchical structure of illocutionary acts within a macro-action can be shown in Fig. 4.3.

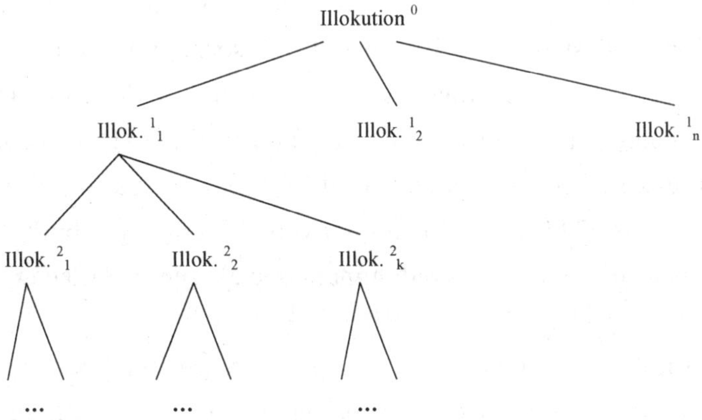

Fig. 4.3 The hierarchical structure of illocutionary acts within a macro-action

As Motsch and Viehweger state in 1981 that any sequence of speech acts must have a global illocutionary act to indicate the intention of all. This illocutionary act is the dominant illocution with the others of subsidiary function supporting it. Thus, the role of discourse in linguistic communication can be concluded as a sequence of specific speech acts has its dominant function of purpose which is determined by the dominant illocutionary act in the discourse. (qtd. in Qian, Minru 48—49) Eventually, discourse is considered as a macro-action with specific speech acts to support it.

Furthermore, there are two points to be noted. One is that the component or compound events are both concepts of relativity. An event may be called compound, since it is composed of the other component events. Meanwhile, it may be also a component if it is used to compose a compound event. The other one is that the component events in a compound event are not only linearly ordered but also related by dependence.

It seems that the action organization much depends on experience and knowledge.

The macro-speech act is recognized without much conscious inference but automatically fixed as a routine. Thus, theoretically, the cognitive operations for obtaining macro-actions are similar to those of propositional information reduction.

The application of results from the philosophy of language such as the view of speech act tells us that by speaking we do something. By a discourse we get a macro-action with a particular purpose. The view to take discourse as controlled and dominated by a global illocutionary act implies that "most of our activities have social implications and our acts are therefore often part of interactions". (van Dijk, *Text and Context: Exploration in the Semantics and Pragmatics of Discourse* 185)

The insight into the nature of language as social semiotic encourages us to assume that the use of language is not only some simple collection of specific acts or a certain macro-action, but an integral part of social interaction greatly influenced and developed by the social system and structure. It is a kind of social interaction since a collective agents involved must have conventions about what should be done in particular situations within a given sociocultural background to realize a certain goal. The conventions usually exist for large groups for an indefinite period of time, at many places, and for many interactions. (Ibid. 187) This is the functional view of language, both as a system and as an historical product, in which the predominant social role of language in interaction is stressed. (Ibid. 167)

The view of speech act provides the possibility to put individual speech act into the more global social surroundings so as to encourage us to study on the more global speech acts and its corresponding more global macro-structure in a pragmatic way. Although the complex macro-action is also hierarchically organized with sequences of actions at various levels by the macro-rules, there is the difference between action and proposition. Propositions are organized at all levels into the macro-structure by meanings, while actions can be organized into the macro-structure of actions by functions which can be represented as macro-categories. The categories imply the social interaction with agents involved realizing their functions to reach a goal. So, the categories are closely associated with types of macro-actions with particular purposes, indicating macro-actions bear some conventional properties according to the functions in the macro-structure of actions. The macro-structure of actions with different categories for different macro-action is called as super-structures or schemata. In some sense, the super-structure is a sort of overall syntax to arrange speech acts into categories according to their functions or roles in realizing a certain goal.

Thus, we may well assume that there is a kind of social events performing as the most global speech acts. This kind of social events can represent social conventions with conventional and overall action syntax to realize a particular goal. The counterpart of the social event in the language system, we can find, is genre. And in this respect, genre is the most global macro-speech act with overall action syntax for a particular intention represented by a certain goal or purpose.

4.2.4 Elements of Macro-Speech Act Potentials

What we discuss above is based on the assumption that using language is a kind of action. As Humboldt states that language in nature is long lasting as well as instantaneous. Any words are incompletely and statically reserved, thus they need to be interpreted again. Language itself is not a product but an activity. (qtd. in Qian Minru 50) The view of language as activity is to settle the intension of between subjects and objects or reality of the world, the key of which lies in the belief that subjects consciously have influences on objects by the medium of subjects' practices or activities.

In this section, we use the notion of macro-speech act to refer to genre with the intention to emphasize the property of action of genre, which implies the importance of the role of genre user or subjects of activity of genre.

4.2.4.1 Purpose of Macro-Speech Act

If someone wants something, he or she may take some actions to realize it. Under a certain cultural background, he or she has a set of knowledge about what types of actions can probably result in such consequence as he or she wants. In this sense, his or her desire transforms into the purpose of action. That is, a purpose is a state of mind in which I have a representation of a wanted future state of affairs or event together with the instruction that this goal must be brought about by an action. (van Dijk, *Text and Context: Exploration in Semantics and Pragmatics of Discourse* 179)

With the constraints of socioculture, a range of language resources is chosen or a certain macro-speech act is done to reach a goal. Therefore, the genre used to reach the goal in language is accepted as a "goal-oriented social process". The purpose of the action or communicative purpose decides the function of genre. For example, the general function of legislation is directive, to impose obligations and to confer rights, since legal draftsman attempts to define the model world of obligations and rights, permissions and prohibitions as precisely, clearly and unambiguously as linguistic resources permit. (Bhatia, *Analysing Genre: Language Use in Professional Settings* 102) In this generic event, there are several component events with their own purposes, including guarding against wriggling out of obligations, protecting rights, trying to include all possibilities in the world and using precise and unambiguous language. But there is a global purpose of the compound event and the purpose of the macro-speech act that is to define the model world of obligations and rights. In other words, what we talk about the purpose of action refers to the communicative purpose of macro-speech act rather than of the specific component events within it. It is true that the global purpose of a macro-speech act decides the function of genre, thus it can be a criteria to define a genre. As Swales' definition of genre states, "communicative purpose is both a privileged criterion and one that operates to keep the scope of a genre as here conceived narrowly focused on comparable rhetorical action". (*Genre Analysis* 58)

The rules we apply to get the purpose of a compound event are similar to those we can use to get the macro-speech act, since macro-speech acts are related to macro-purposes.

There are two points worthwhile to note. First, the global purpose to define a genre is constrained by socioculture in the parent discourse community. That is to say, "the purposes are recognized by the expert members of the parent discourse community". Actually, it is by discourse communities that the "genre names can be inherited" and "produced and imported by others to constitute valuable ethnographic communication". (Ibid.) The generic intertextuality does occur during the process. In this sense, the global purposes are socioculture-oriented purposes. "The expert members of the discourse community to achieve private intentions within the framework of socially recognized purpose(s)." (Bhatia, *Analyzing Genre* 13)

Second, purpose is closely linked with the notion of interaction. On the one hand, purpose is ultimately a state of mind. Specifically, the author's intention is implied in the purpose of communicating with the audience. On the other hand, the global purpose as socioculture-oriented purpose also implies the interaction amongst users. It means that author's purpose must be recognized and accepted by the audience within a certain socioculture. And only when the purpose can be recognized and accepted by the audience, the purpose can be taken as the criteria to define a genre. Hence some elements used to realize the purpose should be highlighted.

The link between action and purpose lies in the plan of action. We assume that the plan of action is needed for the purpose of action. In other words, plans are the key to link action and it purpose.

Given a certain purpose, the agent may choose a course of action to realize a maximum of the goal. To fulfill it, he or she may "form a particular intention of action or a plan of action, to be executed in a specific situation". (van Dijk, *Text and Context: Exploration in the Semantics and Pragmatics of Discourse* 180)

In the functional view, the notion of plan can be understood as stage or move, as Martin states that "[...] staged because it usually takes us a few steps to reach our goal". (Martin and Rose 7) Still in the field of systemic functional linguistics, Eggins and Slade illustrate that a genre is staged as the meanings are made in steps, it usually takes more than one step for participants to achieve their goals; a genre is goal oriented in that texts typically move through stages to a point of closure, and are considered incomplete if the culmination is not reached; genre are negotiated interactively and are the realization of a social purpose. (56)

As to the moves or stages in the most global macro-speech act, rich achievements have been got. Some of them are story grammar, generic structures, and textual patterns or text structure, etc.

4.2.4.2 Super-Structure

According to what we discussed above, the differences of macro-structures that depend on different language users or in different pragmatic contexts or social situations can imply that macro-structures may in turn be subject to certain rules and constraints for different genres. The differences do not lie in the form of the hierarchical structure or its macro-rules, but lie in the categories to which macro-propositions in macro-structure are assigned to represent specific functions of component events within the macro-action. The hierarchical structure with the categories is called as super-structure.

In this sense, super-structure is a kind of overall syntax which defines the possible forms in which topics or themes are ordered by their functions in a given macro-action. The overall syntax is born with the action logics which show the implied social conventions for a large group for an indefinite period of time, at many places, and for many interactions. Thus, super-structure is of genre rather than discourse.

The most well developed super structure is probably story grammar. Mandler et al. presented stories that are coherent from the standpoint of the story grammar to a sample group of children and adults in Liberia. Liberia is a country in northern Africa in which formal education is not required and the participants of course varied in their degree of literacy and education. Some had no formal education and were not literate, some had some degree of school experience but could not read, and still some were both schooled and literate. The results for these groups as well as comparable U. S. Groups can be shown in Fig. 4.4.

The left side of the figure shows recall patterns for U. S. and Liberian adults, and the right side shows children's recall. Clearly, there is a great similarity in the recall patterns. All groups recalled settings, beginnings, attempts, and outcomes better than reactions and endings. Children in both cultures show a low level of recall, but the patterns are similar. These results suggest that a story grammar of the type described by Mandler and others could be a universal schema rather than one that is specific to one

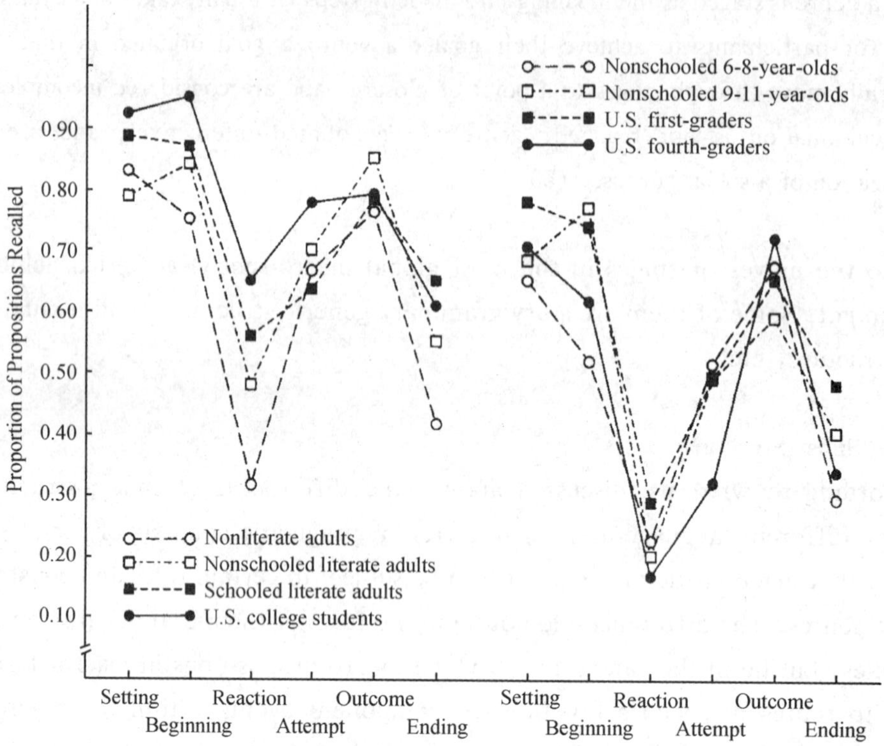

Fig. 4.4 Proportion of propositions recalled from story constituents by different populations (qtd. in Carroll 181)

culture. Also, it is suggested that this does not mean that no culture differences exist in story schemata, but then the certain schemata are culturally invariant. This is the famous story grammar which supports that there are some set moves in the form of a universal schema for the action of story. It encourages us to boldly convince that there are always moves for different macro-speech act. And further studies on it flourish.

The studies on genre of narrative are greatly influenced by story grammar. A narrative may express several narrative structures, but such a proposition may have a function within it as a whole. There may be the category of setting for events and actions to indicate time, place or other circumstances of a certain episode, or even to introduce the characters; the category of complication and resolution defining the episode of the story, which may be followed by an evaluation and a moral.

Another most convincing example is that in the field of news. According to the analysis of the thematic structures of a few news items, van Dijk tries to give a hypothetical structure of a news schema and further news schema categories as Fig. 4.5.

This figure involves all the possible categories existing theoretically. And not all of the possible categories but only some of them will be contained in many news texts. In most cases, the headline and main events are obligatory in a minimally well-formed news

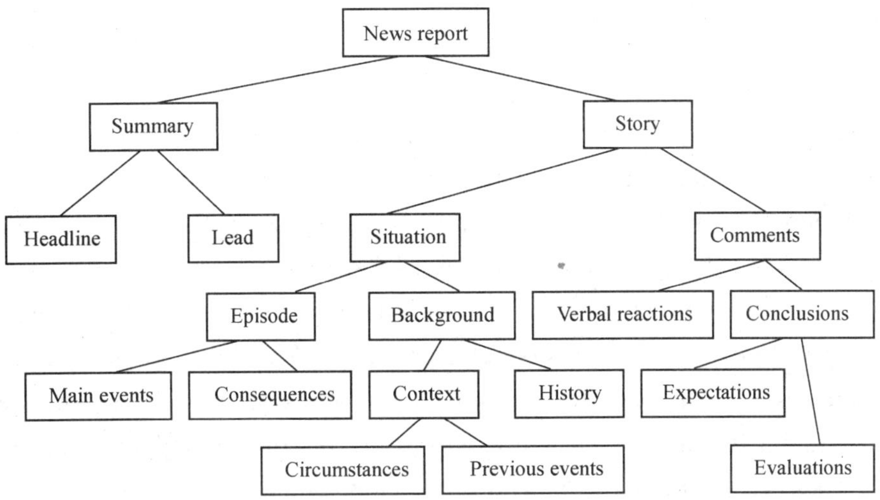

Fig. 4.5 Hypothetical structure of a news schema (*News as Discourse* 55)

discourse, while the other categories are optional. On the other hand, some categories may be repeated in the same news discourse. What's more, the ordering of these categories can not be definitely set. Because of the other factors such as relevance and news values, the order can be changed. That is to say, the general relevance principle is more powerful than the basic top-down strategy that the higher level information of each category must be first realized. And sometimes to achieve the news values, some adaptations of ordering of categories in news production can also occur.

The super-structure actually sets the conventional rules and social constraints for macro-structure. The conventional rules and social constraints are all determined by the social events of genres. The super-structure which is realized by macro-rules with macro-propositions assigned in its categories can be regarded as patterns of meaning which are relatively consistent for each genre. That is to say, the types of categories and rules determining the overall organization of a discourse at the same time identify the types of discourses involved. For example, in a narrative, the macro-rules are able to explicitly link the sequence of sentences of a story with the particular narrative categories or functions. Without the narrative categories we could produce a linguistically acceptable, ie an interpretable discourse, but such a discourse would have no "point". (van Dijk, *Text and Context: Exploration in the Semantics and Pragmatics of Discourse* 154) In other words, no function can be located within a discourse without generic categories.

In the functional perspective, genre is a staged, goal-oriented social process. Thus, patterns of meaning for a given genre are to reflect the plan of the genre to realize its purpose of action. It is by the patterns that we can learn to predict how each situation is likely to unfold, and learn how to interact in a certain genre as a social process. (Martin and Rose 7) All of these become the theoretical basis of the elements of our hypothetical macro-speech act potentials.

4.2.4.3 Generic Structure

The privileging of purpose goes along with a view of genre analysis as primarily concerned with "staging", differentiating genres in terms of their generic structure. Analysis of generic structure is of valuable for purpose-driven genres. (Fairclough, *Analysing Discourse: Textual Analysis for Social Research* 72)

Although it seems impossible to give a definite generic structure for a certain genre, it is still helpful to explore the possible elements in an activity of genre, showing us the potential courses we can take to accomplish a macro-speech act. In this sense, the analysis of staging or generic structure is a study on the possible ritualized language activity in society. As Fairclough says, "the more ritualized an activity is, the more relevant such an analysis is". (Ibid.) And it supports the necessity of studying generic structure potentials rather than specific generic structure.

As to generic structure potential, Hasan is the first one who proposes the concept. Studies of generic structure potentials mainly focuses on the four respects. What are the obligatory elements for a generic structure? What are the optional elements? In what sequence are the elements of generic structure? And whether there are elements of recurrence? For example, by the research on the quiet ritualized mundane market transactions, Hasan concludes its generic structure possibly contains such elements as greeting, sales initiation, sale enquiry, sales request, sales compliance, sale, purchase, purchase closure and finis. The generic structure potential can be shown as follows:

> [(Greeting)? (Sales Initiation) ^] [↵ (Sales Enquiry?) ^ {Sales Request ^ ↵ Sales Compliance} ^ Sale] ^ Purchase ^ Purchase Closure (^ Finis) (Hu, Zhuanglin, Zhu, Yongsheng, 289)

In this generic structure potential, some elements are obligatory, such as sales enquiry, sale and purchase; while others are optional, such as sales initiation. Some elements are in a fixed sequence; while other elements are flexibly ordered. Some elements are adjacent as marked with " ^ ". Some elements marked with "↵" can occur multiple times at different locations.

Hasan's research arouses great attention and is much influential in the studies of genre, although she has been greatly criticized for failing in defining genre appropriately and identifying the register with genre. Greatly influenced by Hasan, Martin focuses on three families of genres: story, argument and legislation in his book *Working with Discourse: Meaning beyond the Clause*. According to his analysis, in a story, there are the relatively stable components of its organization such as orientation, incident, interpretation and coda. In an argument, the elements are thesis, argument with grounds and conclusion. And in the genre of legislation, the generalizable stages are purpose, motivation and provision which can be further divided into definition and actual provision.

Also in the domain of functionalism, Ventola and Eggins do the similar studies on generic structure. The greatest contribution made by Eggins is to distinguish two criteria, the criteria of form and the criteria of function. According to the two criteria, we can analyze the elements in different ways. Elements can be organized by form or by function. Take the academic genre for example, if we analyze the elements of the generic structure by form, the elements can be chapter one, chapter two, and so on. But if we analyze it by function, the elements are usually introduction, body and conclusion. Generally speaking, the form criteria focuses on the similarity among the elements of genre, and the function criteria stresses the differences among them. (Ibid. 290)

The studies in specific generic structure potentials are rich in various domains. Swales gets the academic and research generic structure; Bhatia researches the generic patterns in promotional genre, Cameron the rigid staging of standard call speech, etc. Take Bhatia's study in the generic patterns in promotional genre for example. In "Generic Patterns in Promotional Discourse", Bhatia proposes that the most traditional form of promotional discourse is found in advertisement. Without going into any detailed generic and discoursal specification of the general advertising genre, Bhatia points out that most printed advertisements of hard sell type make use of some of the following rhetorical moves to persuade potential customers to buy the product or service they promote. The generic structure for advertisement in terms of rhetorical moves is as follows:

1. Headlines
2. Targeting the market
3. Justifying the product or service by establishing a niche
4. Detailing the product or service
5. Establishing credentials
6. Endorsement or Testimonials
7. Offering incentives
8. Using pressure tactics
9. Soliciting response
10. Signature line and logo etc.

All of these studies well support the assumption that genres have their corresponding generic structures. And the generic structure is a typical property of genre. Thus, it is a very important potential for generic intertextuality.

4.2.4.4 Text Structure or Textual Pattern

The notion of text structure or textual pattern is mostly discussed by defining its categories and illustrating its importance. Michael Hoey argues that readers seem to bring two kinds of knowledge to bear on the texts they read — the specific knowledge described by schemata and scripts and a more generalized set of expectations that are shared across a range of texts. (*Textual Interaction: An Introduction to Written Discourse Analysis* 122)

Eugene Winter suggests that there is a kind of basic text structure as a vehicle for systemically settling for saying less than everything on a strict relevance principle. ("Clause Relations as Information Structure: Two Basic Text Structures in English" 56) He gives an example to illustrate the role of sequence and an awareness of its meaningful units in the structuring of a basic text or message. He asks someone to choose one sequence only in answer to the question: "which one of the six patterns shown below represents the actual sequence observed on a street poster which was advertising *The Harpenden Weekly News*?" the choices of sequences are as follow:

(a) Enjoy it. Buy it. Read it.
(b) Buy it. Enjoy it. Read it.
(c) Read it. Enjoy it. Buy it.
(d) Enjoy it. Read it. Buy it.
(e) Buy it. Read it. Enjoy it.
(f) Read it. Buy it. Enjoy it.

In Britain, the result of the experiment is that all choose the fifth sequence, because it corresponds with the cultural expectation about the time sequence in which a newspaper is habitually bought and read. By the experiment, Winter concludes three points:

(1) In a three-element structure like this, the first is potentially the 'beginning' and the last is potentially the 'end'.

(2) The culturally familiar situation of obtaining newspapers is compressed into the actions of the first two clauses, and their evaluation is expressed by the last clause.

(3) The three imperative clauses are in the relation of 'weak logical sequence' of simple narrative time with each other, where each event is assumed to follow the other in time. (Ibid.)

The analysis leads to a belief that there should be some consensus principles about typical message structure or texts. The consensus principle shown by the experiment is only one of them. Accordingly, three common forms of consensus principles are proposed by Winter. They are Situation and Evaluation, Hypothetical and Real, and combinations of both. These text structures are actually to imply the logic underlying the surface message structure. And the moves of message development and organization in cognition are explicitly presented.

As to the patterns of message structure, many studies have been conducted by other scholars also. One of the most outstanding is Michael Hoey. In his *Textual Interaction: An Introduction to Written Discourse Analysis*, he uses the term "organization" rather than "structure" to indicate the patterns of message structure. Hoey holds although there are preferred sequences and combinations of elements, there is no impossible sequence or combination. However, text organization is culturally popular considering that they do not have a universal status but occur within particular cultures. Within a given culture, some of the patterns are very rare while others will recur with great frequency. (122—123) Hoey lists some of the culturally popular patterns of text organization, including the problem-solution pattern, the goal-achievement pattern, the opportunity-taking pattern, the desire arousal-fulfillment pattern, and the gap in knowledge-filling pattern, etc. When he tries to apply these patterns to practical teaching, he states:

> From a practical teaching point of view, several of the specific patterns are of special importance. The goal-achievement pattern and the gap in knowledge-filling pattern just described are particularly valuable for people learning to read and / or write in English in an academic context, since both patterns are widely used in academic writing. Goal-achievement and opportunity-taking are both widely used in business English. Only the desire-arousal pattern has relatively little functional importance from a writing perspective, though it occurs widely in the kinds of leisure text that learners of English might read and, of course, slightly indirectly, account for many advertisements. (*Textual Interaction: An Introduction to Written Discourse Analysis* 168—169)

His statements clarifies the closely relation between genres and text patterns. Some text patterns are much more popular for some genres within some sociocultures. Since the text patterns are the forms of message organization to realize the interaction between message producers and message receivers and the author has a purpose in communicating to the audience, the author may well choose a most effective way to realize his goal or purpose of the communication. Furthermore, usually a communication is intended for more than one person. Sharing the same socioculture, the audience has much knowledge of choosing what course and taking what moves to reach the purpose or goal in common. Thus, text patterns can be understood as the most effective courses with the corresponding moves according to their purposes of communication within a certain socioculture.

4.3 Evaluation Potentials

Since Halliday suggests functional approaches to grammar and equates meaning with function, one of the metafunctions — the interpersonal metafunction has been greatly focused. Evaluation in the communication is mainly about the writer or speaker's attitude or feelings about what he or she is talking about. It is believed that evaluation can not only express personal or collective value systems, but also can build and maintain a relationship with the hearer or reader. In this sense, evaluation involves interpersonal meaning and it has surely received increasing attention. The necessity of studying evaluation has a lot supported. As Vološinov states

> any word used in actual speech possesses not only theme and meaning in the referential, or content, sense of these words, but also value judgment: i. e., all referential contents produced in living speech are said or written in conjunction with a specific evaluative accent. There is not such thing as word without evaluative accent. (103)

Accordingly, we argue that genre as macro-speech act can never be without evaluative sense and born with evaluation, which leads to the assumption that evaluation can be a very important potential for generic intertextuality. In this section, we try to discuss how evaluation can be realized in generic intertextuality. Specifically speaking, what is the relation between social-oriented evaluation and generic intertextuality. In our discussion, the role relationships or positions are to be fully focused since we believe the evaluation system is in some sense represented by them. As Halliday explains,

> The langue we use caries according to the level of formality, of technicality, and so on. What is the variable underlying this type of distinction? Essentially, it is the role relationships in the situation in question: who the participants in the communication group are, and in what relationship they stand to each other. (qtd. in Hatim, *Communication across Culture* 26)

4.3.1 Evaluation

In SFL, the theory of evaluation has been developed very well. Most outstanding ones are probably Martin, White and Rose. In their studies, evaluation is discussed in terms of appraisal which "is concerned with evaluation: the kinds of attitudes that are negotiated in a text, the strength of the feeling involved and the ways in which values are sourced and readers aligned". (Martin and Rose 22) So, the presumption for appraisal theory is to consider any language communication as interactive, thus there is always negotiation. The key of the interaction is attitudes involving feelings and values. In this sense, attitudes become the most important respect of evaluative resources. Since attitudes have to do with evaluating things, people's character and their feelings, there are three main types of attitudes: expressing emotion, judging character and valuing the worth of things. Technically, expressing feelings is referred as affect, judging character as judgment and valuing the worth of things as appreciation. According to White, (qtd. in Li Zhanzi 286—292) affect is a kind of emotional responses such as happiness, sadness, pride, fear, etc.; judgment refers to a series of norms for moral evaluations of behavior, by which behaviors can be judged as ethical or not, legal or not, acceptable or not, etc.; and appreciation is about views of value on more abstract semiotic processes and natural phenomena, thus to set up the aesthetic quality such as dramatic, innovative, harmonious, etc.

Besides attitude, there are the other two respects of evaluative resources in the whole appraisal systems. They are engagement and graduation. Graduation is to show to which extend evaluation can be intense or attitude can be amplified. It includes force and focus involving respectively the resources to raise or lower the intensity of attitude and the options of sharpening or softening the semantic focuses of evaluation. And engagement is concerned with attitude's source, considering the attitude may be the writer or speaker's own or it may be others'. If it comes from other voices, the source can be realized by projection, modalization and concession. The overview of whole appraisal systems can be shown as Fig. 4.6:

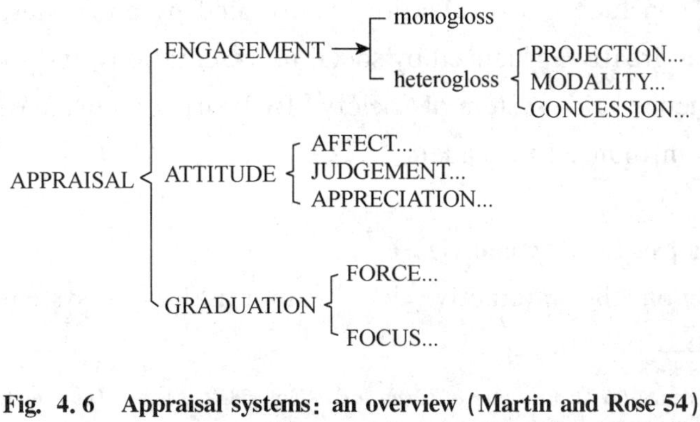

Fig. 4.6 Appraisal systems: an overview (Martin and Rose 54)

4.3.2 Social-Oriented Evaluation and Generic Intertextuality

4.3.2.1 Evaluation and Social Representation

Evaluation is generally about one's opinion, showing one's view of value from a value system. Considering value systems must be in the form of social representation, we argue that evaluation is social-oriented. Social representation is a tendency of culture and ideology, nothing to do with specific situational contexts. It is a collective consciousness shared by a certain society with a certain culture or social and culturally specific knowledge. Social representation can not be achieved by our own daily experiences as knowledge of background, but greatly by the media of language.

Anderson once made a social survey. He found that almost all of the white hold the belief that the black are lazy, stupid, superstitious and good at music.① It is worthwhile to notice that a lot of people in the surveyed group have no experiences of having contact with the black and what they know about the black is totally got from the mass media and social ideologies. Gradually, the belief that the black are lazy, stupid, superstitious becomes a bias for the whole society.

Scollon made another experiment to support the idea of social representation. In his experiment, he showed a picture to two groups of American children. On the picture there was a wide road with two rows of trees on each side. To the first group of children, he told them that the picture was taken in America and asked them what could be behind the trees. The group of children answered that there might be farms. When he showed the same picture to the other group of children, he told them that the picture was taken in Russia and raised the same question. Then the children guessed there might be a military base.② Obviously, the American children have established the pattern idea about the two countries, which is later proven to be formed due to the information delivered by language from parents, teachers, newspapers, televisions, etc.

Thus, we can conclude that evaluation determined by one's view of value must be social-oriented. It is greatly influenced by social representation, and social representation is expected to influence value system of society. By bearing an evaluative accent, a value system behind it is introduced to readers.

4.3.2.2 Social Subject Identity and Genre

What's more, on the interactive basis, appraisal is a system of interpersonal

---

① See J. R. Anderson, *The architecture of Cognition* (Cambridge, Mass.: Harvard University Press, 1983), qtd. in 熊学亮,认知语言学概论(上海:上海外语教育出版社,2000) 116.

② See R. Scollon, *Conversations with a one year old child* (Honolulu: University of Hawaii Press, 1776), qtd. in 熊学亮,认知语言学概论(上海:上海外语教育出版社,2000) 116.

meanings which can be used for negotiating our social relationships. (Martin and Rose 22) That is to say, evaluation is the key which should be focused on, if we want to fully understand the rhetorical potential or communicative property of a certain type of discourse or genre. And evaluative accent shows the strategy the writer or speaker takes to be consensus with the reader or hearer, by which a kind of social subject identity is set up.

In this sense, genre as macro-speech act in a certain society with a certain culture must be closely relevant to evaluation, since genre can neither value-free nor neutral and they strategically embody attitudes, values, and ways of doing. (Coe et al. 3) Thus, genre can be defined by evaluation. Or evaluation can be criteria of genre decision. Some genres such as forewords, book reviews, and editorials are all characterized by their evaluative traits. Hence usually they can be diverse in the form of sub-genre in the genre colonies.

For example, in administrative correspondence there are a number of establishable genres, two of which are the individually-directed "good news" letter and "bad news" letter. (qtd. in Swales, *Genre Analysis: English in Academic and Research Settings* 53) These two closely related genres are thought to be the same as they are all responses to applications. But they can be treated differently considering the assumptions of their information are different in terms of evaluation. The good news letter is assumed to transmit the welcomed information, while the bad news is based on the assumption that the information is unwelcome.

Thus, we can conclude that evaluation is realized in genre by the social subject identity of participants through the system of values in the society with a certain culture. The ideologies of genres simultaneously generate social representation and organize human beings into communities.

Kress provides a convincing example. (qtd. in Fairclough, *Discourse and Social change* 133—134) He analyzes samples of educational texts of various types, and suggests that their generic intertextuality incorporates elements shared with genre of advertisement by subject position transformation. For example, advertisements for household cleaning agents share with school textbooks for home management classes the property of distributing agency in cleaning processes between the human cleaner and the commodity, which suggests in both cases that the human cleaner needs the commodity. Thus, school textbooks, and other forms of educational discourse contribute to the constitution of subjects as consumers, and the educational process appears, amongst other things, to educate readers to read advertisements.

The example shows the relevance to the constitution of social groups and communities, as well as to the socialization of individuals. Obviously, such discursive practices simultaneously generate a consumerist view of the world, and a community of consumers associated with such a view.

However, if we consider the social subject identity as absolute position in a particular society at a particular time, we need to discuss the role of evaluation playing in the activity of genre. In terms of appraisal, the social subject identity determines the value taken to influence the attitude towards world entities or propositions; while the relative social relationship is to set positions for participants. Both of them make contributions to the evaluative sense or conventions of genre. So in the following section, we try to talk about how the construction of position expresses in the activity of genre, and what is the relation between position transformation and generic intertextuality.

4.3.2.3 Position Transformation and Generic Intertextuality

As Xin Bin points out that different genres have their own ways to construct subject positions. (*Critical Linguistics: Theory and Application* 143) Every genre must construct the roles and positions for its participants. (Ibid. 140) The positions of participants not only refer to subject position but also reading position. The subject position is set for the user of genre and the reading position is for the interpreter of genre. The two kinds of positions are complementary. Users of genres are to construct positions for readers, meanwhile the construction of reading position is to enhance the subject position. In other words, it is the expectations from readers for the conventions of genre activities that encourage the construction of subject positions. The genre activities are thus constrained by positions of participants.

Since the positions of participants in some sense illustrate the conventions of genres and define the genres, the position transformation implies the change of genres or other genres involved. In Xin Bin's words, "different genres have different semantic potentials and set or construct different subject positions, hence generic intertextuality imply the change of subject and construction of different reading position in applying different genres". (Ibid. 143)

In the case of the example of "Using it's simple you don't even have to speak the language" given by Fairclough introduced in 2.3.1 above, two relationships are married. One is the advertiser-consumer relationship, another is the relationship between institution as rule-giver and member of the public, specifically bank and customer. With the change of relationship or the different positions constructed, generic intertextuality can be easily spotted.

Another famous example about position transformation with the occurrence of generic intertextuality comes from Tannen.

(Teasing)

Doctor: That's my light.

Child: / this goes up there. /

Doctor: It goes up there. That's right.

(Reporting)

Now while we're examining her head we're feeling for lymph nodes in her neck ... or for any masses ... okay ... also you palpate the midline for thyroid, for goiter ... if there's any.

(Teasing)

Now let us look in your mouth. Okay? With my light. Can you open up real big? ... Oh, bigger ... Oh bigger ... bigger.

By the analysis shown above, there are obviously two genres in the conversation between the doctor and the child, or there is generic intertexutality. The generic intertextuality happens when the position transformation occurs. According to the former positions, the relationship between speaker and hearer is adult-child; while the latter pair of positions is to set the relationship between adults.

It is worthwhile to note that the construction of reading position can also serve as an element for recognition of genre by helping to strengthen the subject position. Here is an example quoted in Xin Bin's *Critical Linguistics: Theory and Application*,

> The area round a town is which its urban functions exert a strong influence can be described as a functional region. In highly urbanized countries this is probably the most useful way of division of large areas into smaller units for study. We need to remember, however, that the boundary of a region can be defined precisely only in terms of one factor, and then only ir that factor can be expressed as a quantity. We can talk of part of northern New South Wales as within the region of 50 per cent or more commercial orientation to Brisbane; we can also talk of that part where 50 per cent or more of the people take in Brisbane daily newspaper; the boundaries are different, but they both mean something precise. To speak of the 'Brisbane region' without any indication of the way it is defined is vague indeed. In Chapter 2 the boundary of a population density region is defined from statistics in a precise way.
>
> We have seen too that functional regions overlap and nest one within another. The fringe zones of the four New Zealand towns in Fig. 5. 8 would overlap one another if plotted on one map. If the criteria used had been comparison rather than convenience goods, it is probable that all four towns would have come within the functional regions of Hamilton, a much larger town. Hamiton, in turn, in other fields could be considered part of the functional region of Auckland, the largest city in New

Zealand. (141)

The pragmatic function of some linguistic skills in the example above is evidently to lead students to seat in the reading position and recognize the genre by accepting the subject position. For example, some linguistic skills expressed with "to speak of" "most useful way of division" "units for study" "can be described" "can be defined" "can be expressed" "it is defined" "was defined statistics" "we need to remember" "in chapter 2 the boundary" "we have seen to", etc, successfully invite students to take the perspective as scientists and construct the reading position with social identity as scientists. By doing that, students accept the subject position of the genre and take the same attitudes of the subjects of the genre to participate evaluation. In this way, the construction of reading position is also important in genre activities in evaluative sense.

So, conclusively speaking, because of the transformation of positions, both subject position and reading position, the generic intertextuality occurs.

4.3.3 Summary

Evaluation involving interpersonal meaning must be a fundamental perspective in the activity of genre. Or genre as macro-speech act can never be without evaluative sense and born with evaluation. Accordingly, we assume that evaluation can be a very important potential for generic intertextuality.

Evaluation can be expressed in two ways. One is absolute social subject identity which is set up by the system of values in the form of social representation. It greatly influences one's evaluation, and the decision of choosing genre. The other is construction of two complementary positions, subject position and reading position. The genre activities are constrained by positions of participants, as the positions of participants in some sense illustrate the conventions of genres and define the genres.

On these bases, it is argued that the position transformation implies the change of genres or other genres involved. Specifically speaking, generic intertextuality can help fulfill the transformation of social identity as well as the positions of participants in the perspective of evaluation. Therefore, social identity and position of participants are the possible elements of evaluation potentials of generic intertextuality. By the transformation of either of them, we can accomplish a process of generic intertextuality.

4.4 Modality Potentials

In the section 3.2.4, we have argued that genre should be taken as macro social semiosis system. In the language system, genre is located on the highest plane. At the same time, genre is monitored and in turn influences ideologies. Or genre is born with the sociocultural sense. Thus, if we interpret genre in the context of socioculture and attach genre with socioculture, we must accept the assumption that a social reality or a culture is itself an edifice of meanings — a semiotic construct. In this perspective, language is one of the semiotic systems that constitute a culture; one that is distinctive in that it also serves as an encoding system for many of the others. That is to say, culture itself is an information system and needs to be interpreted in semiotic terms. (Halliday, *Language as Social Semiotic: The Social Interpretation of Language and Meaning* 2)

In this sense, genre as macro social semiosis system or social practice is not only interpreted by socioculture but also participates in the construction of socioculture. Culture is a collective system of socially meaningful practices and correlates with genre. The social practice not only involves language but can be also realized by any practices in the abstract forms of semiosis. It is consensus with statement that "thought follows the material state of signs". (Beaugrande, *Linguistic Theory: The Discourse of Fundamental Works* 10) And furthermore, it settles the paradox in Saussure's view that on one hand "language exists independently of the material substance of words" and "a material sign is not necessary for the expression of an idea", and on the other hand "abstract entities are always based on concrete entities". (Ibid.)

On this basis, the study of multimodality draws great attention. From the very beginning of discourse analysis, it has been well accepted that discourse is multiply structured. In the functional linguistics, Halliday and others emphasize that language as social semiotic realizes many functions simultaneously in a certain society within a certain culture. The attention to multi-modal discourse is in some sense enhanced by the traditional view, especially considering the belief that different semiotic resources or dimensions fulfill different communicative functions.

4.4.1 Mode, Modality and Multimodality

The word "modality" comes from the word "mode". It differs from the "modality" in English grammar which is more closely relevant to the "model" in the "model verb". In terms of register in SFL, mode refers to what part language is playing, what it is that the participants are expecting language to do for them in the situation: the symbolic organization of the text, the status that it has, and its function in the context. (Halliday and Hasan 12)

Mode makes it possible for us to focus on the extra-linguistic contexts in another way. When Martin and Rose talk about the mode in *Working with Discourse: Meaning beyond the Clause* in which the exophoric reference in Lingiari's speech is treated as context dependent, they propose to take another perspective to study discourse. There are more than one modality involved. "Using the term modality here in the sense of a modality of communication such as language, music, image or action". It actually suggests that "we need to expand our conception of mode to embrace multimodal discourse analysis", which "entails going beyond linguistics into social semiotics and taking into account as many modalities of communication as we can systematically describe". (Martin and Rose 255)

In this way, we understand multimodality as a new horizon to study social communicative activities. In a more macro perspective, communication is more than language itself, thus language study should be extended to include any other non-linguistic semiotic systems for delivering meaning. These semiotic systems can be any physical systems of representation, such as performance art, sign language, gesture, painting, sculpture, photography, design, music and film. Generally speaking, multimodality is the combination of several modalities. And all types of discourses can be multimodal in the sense that spoken language is always accompanied by paralinguistic means of communication such as speech-sound, rhythm, intonation, facial expression, gesture and posture, and that written language is always also a visual arrangement of marks on a page. (Anthonissen 299)

In functional linguistics, multimodality discourse analysis has been a frontier with achievements on the studies of image, music, sound and action alongside language. For example, in the domain of written discourses, Kress and Leeuwen have considered semiotic modes other than language that in various kinds of discourses, which has resulted in their comprehensive theory of visual communication. To illustrate, they consider how images, as a semiotic mode alternative to language, are used in a variety of texts, such as children's books, science textbooks and newspaper front pages. And they even develop theoretical tools with which to describe and explain the perceived order and regularity in visual communication.

4.4.2 Multimodality and Generic Intertextuality

As Lemke holds, words corresponds to the language semiotic resources while social semiotics contain much more than language semiotic resources. Thus the construction of social semiotics can refer to all kinds of meanings expressed by any social semiotic resources, such as gestures in speaking, diagrams in writing and so on. "We use language, in conjunction with other semiotic resource systems and their associated social practices (drawing, gesturing, etc.) to construct multiple social realities." (Lemke, "Interpersonal Meaning in Discourse: Value Orientations" 83) In this sense, besides the genres confined within the domain of language semiotic resource, there should be an action genre realized by other modalities rather than language.

Lemke's view is also supported by others, such as Thibault, Kress and Baldry, and so on. They all agree that all of modalities play the same role as language serving as social semiotic resource systems that are formed in society and carry meanings. In other words, we need a complementary account of the social semiotic resource systems that are available to the members of the community — the systems of relations of semiotic forms of all kinds to their possible meanings. (Thibault, "Contextualization and Social Meaning-making Practices" 43) Baldry even proposes that any social semiotic resources can realize the three meta-functions as language, and meanings are the integrity of meanings by multimodality. (qtd. in Hu, ZhuangLin, "Multimodalization in Social Semiotics" 6)

As to what is the relationship between modality and genre or how modality is involved in given genres, we argue that the involvement of any modality can bring about meanings into genre activity. As Kress and Leeuwen present that different semiotic modes, visual, verbal or gestural, each have their potentialities and limitations, different modes may be more or less useful for different matters that are to be represented. (qtd. in Anthonissen 301) For example, it is probable that when a shift from verbal to visual occurs, a new world is created as visually represented. By adding the new world, new meanings and functions are introduced since visual images may serve as indirect verbal representation.

Take the multimodal coffee-table-sized edition, the *Illustrated Long Walk to Freedom* for example. In this edition, words are accompanied by one or more glossy black-and-white or color photographs on every two-page spread, a radical contrast to the 1995 edition which is mainly writing, except for the few black-and-white photos grouped together in the middle of the book. In this case, the political change recontextualizing spiritual development in the multimodal text is implicitly presented by images and marginalia. By the object of the crowd's gaze to the previous page and through Madela's reincarnation as the young boy born with a hunger to be free, the political change is shown that a white supremacist regime is to be replaced with a non-racial democratic one. His humility is recontextualized as a graceful retirement. (Martin and Rose 255—262)

In the perspective of appraisal, other modalities involved such as images have tremendous attitudinal impact. That is what has been discussed as

> Texts can be multiply structured in other ways, if they show multiple voicing or heteroglossia. Texts often reflect and recycle different voices, which may be realized through different modalities or indeed a single modality, and addressing one or many audiences. (Jaworski and Coupland 8)

For example, David Graddol's study of a wine label illustrates how the label, as a "semiotic space", consists of different sub-texts, realized in different visual fonts and layout. The sub-texts give a description of the type of wine and its qualities, a health warning, and a bar and numerical code. Many of them realize different voices — consumerist, legal, commercial. They address potentially different audiences — consumers, health promoters, retailers — and for different reasons. (Ibid.)

Since different semiotic resources or dimensions fulfill different communicative functions, genre as macro social semiosis system can be multi-modal. If a configuration of genre shows as a set of social practices which make meanings, the genre produced in this process is multi-modal, since more than one semiotic system is applied. For example, a television commercial may combine any of the following elements: spoken and written language, still and moving images, live actors and animation / computer graphics, music, etc.

Thus, if we take a macro perspective and regard genre a macro social semiosis system, as we argue in the Chapter Three, generic intertextuality can be realized by involvement of multimodalities. When modality is interfered in an action genre, it has been accepted as a semiotic system. Considering the other semiotic systems of modalities probably co-articulate meaning with language, multimodality implies a kind of generic intertextuality. For example, in our daily newspaper, magazines, advertisements, children's story books, textbooks, selected works, encyclopedia, and instructions leaflets, etc. all involve several modalities. In the simplest words, since modality is an element of genre activity, we may well assume that reference to more than one modality is a kind of generic intertextuality.

4.4.3 Significance of Multimodality Potentials in Generic Intertextuality Research

The study of multimodality potentials in generic itnertextuality has far-reaching significance, as the important role of other modalities such as images, music, and sound, etc. in a wide range of media communication has been noted.

The focus on multimodality potentials is to support and is meanwhile determined by our very beginning assumption that genre is a macro social semiosis system. In a macro view, language is only one of a variety in the whole social semiotic systems, serving as a modality for people to apply in making sense. According to Kress, material media molded by society for long time can be a semantic resource expressing the meanings for different communities and become modalities. Thus, modality is socioculture-oriented. Both meaning and modality are of social property. In this sense, Kress's approach to communication starts from a social base. Meanings expressed by speakers, writers, printmakers, photographers, painters or sculptors are first and foremost social meanings, which arise out of the society in which the individuals live and work. (Anthonissen 301) Therefore, multimodality potential research is to broaden the approach confined within the domain of language semiotic system and lead the research of generic intertextuality to include other modalities. It goes beyond linguistics into social semiotics.

Secondly, the study in multimodality potentials manages to prove the interaction of modalities to be meaningful. As Kress and Leeuwen argue that "the visual component of a text is an independently organized and structured message, connected to the written component, but not necessarily dependent on it", different modalities represent different sets of meaning that are "neither fully conflated, nor entirely opposed". (Kress and Leeuwen 18) What's more, modalities can occur simultaneously and cooperate with each other. And this kind of interaction among modalities is also meaningful. Users of modality can constantly adapt modality by modifying the old modalities or creating the new modalities. For example, a hypothetical car TV commercial may embody a number of "real" or "implied" voices, addressing viewers in a multitude of roles — as drivers, passengers, car experts, status-seekers, parents concerned over their children's safety, overseers of family budgets, etc. The different voices to be heard or seen in this context can be realized via spoken language, e. g. , a matter-of-fact commentary on the merits of the car, such as its safety, its comfort or its favorable price. They may appear through written or visual signs, e. g. , the company's logo or the advertisement's small print. Cinematic and musical elements will also be present, e. g. , photographs representing selected features of the car's design or its appearance and performance on the road, or a well-known tune with "fitting" lyrics, and so on. (Jaworski and Coupland 8) In this case, the involvement of multimodalities itself carries the intention of temptation by implied or indirect voices to avoid the resentment from audience.

In this sense, we argue that multimodality potentials can be fundamental in generic intertextuality system.

4.5 Summary

Up to now, we have discussed possible potentials in generic intertextuality system. They are disciplinary potentials, macro-speech act potentials, evaluation potentials, and modality potentials. Each of them provides a resource for users to choose. When we talk about generic intertextuality, we imply the reference of a certain component in a particular domain of potentials in generic intertextuality system. Actually, it is constant interaction across the domains of potentials that ensures generic intertextuality.

It must be noted that the components in each set of potentials are all organized hierarchically. That is to say, the combination of choices from each set of potentials realizes a genre. But some elements chosen from the potentials are not necessary but optional ones. The optional elements can be shared by some genres but not typical for any one of them. When the essential elements of a certain genre are intertextualized, generic intertextuality occurs. So, studies in generic intertextuality must involve an issue of mechanism. With the help of mechanism, generic intertextuality process can be realized by deciding and choosing from essential elements which are decided by socioculture with certain ideologies. In the following chapter, we are to discuss the process of generic intertextuality.

Chapter Five

Generic Intertextuality Process

As we have mentioned above, our theoretical framework for generic intertexutality research partly comes from Saussure as well as his followers and partly from Peirce's approach. Both of them agree that language is a kind of symbolic sign system which is characterized by being arbitrary, although Saussure never uses the word of symbol. The view implies that on one hand symbolic signs are built up or used as signs for given purposes or conventional designations with a certain meaning because of social conventional usage, and on the other hand language use is a dynamic process with the principle of flexibility as well as the strategies users take to fulfill certain purposes.

On the basis of the beliefs above, we try to borrow the distinction between system and process and apply it to the study of generic intertextuality, following the Peirce's emphasis on semiosis as a process as well as his view of interaction and interpretation. In this sense, generic intertextuality is a kind of system of resources, and meanwhile concerns a dynamic process with interaction and cognition.

What we have discussed in Chapter Four is about the potentials of the system, or what is included in the social semiotic resource system; while what we will refer to in this chapter is about the process of generic intertextuality or how the potentials of the resource system can be chosen from and what is the mechanism of generic intertextuality process.

Generally speaking, generic intertextuality system provides potentials, while the process of generic intertextuality realizes the choice from potentials. Then the problem is what is the mechanism for generic intertextuality process or how the choice from potentials can be realized. The purpose of the chapter is to find the answer to the problems as what is the cognitive mechanism of generic intertextuality, and how can a subject know what to choose from the resources and how to reorganize the information from potentials to realize the process of generic intertextuality. Anyway, we take generic intertextuality process as the configuration of generic intertextuality system.

5.1 Mechanism of Generic Intertextuality Process

Mechanism is respectively defined in *Merriam-Webster's Collegiate Dictionary* as "a process or technique for achieving a result" and in *The Concise Oxford Dictionary of English* as "a system of mutually adapted parts working together in or as in a machine". The two definitions reflect the properties of mechanism from different perspectives. According to the definitions, mechanism can be understood as a system of interactive and cooperated principles and devices with a set goal. Thus, the mechanism of generic intertextuality process may well be considered as a system of closely related principles and devices used to realize the configuration of generic intertextuality system by choosing from the potentials. The mechanism itself shows the dynamic of the process.

Considering the four sets of potentials that we have got totally as components of the semiosis system of generic intertextuality stem from our analysis on register variables as well as their application in a certain socioculture with ideologies by subjects, these potentials may well be recognized by subjects and treated as cognitive representation.

So, we assume that the mechanism of generic intertextuality process must involve cognitive model which can be used to cover all the stored cognitive representation, the configuration of mental spaces and the integration of mental spaces.

5.2 Cognitive Models of Generic Intertextuality Potentials

According to cognitive linguistics, cognitive information processing is the same as the processing of all sorts of other information about the world such as in perception and action. A concept is definable as a configuration of cognitive content which can be recovered or activated with more or less unity and consistency in the mind. (Beaugrande, *Introduction to Text Linguistics* 4)

If we want to understand in what kind of form each set of potentials is organized, we may refer to some basic concepts first. They are cognitive categories and prototypes. Cognitive categories can be understood as mental concepts stored in our mind. They make up what has been called "mental lexicon". According to the classical model, categories come as homogeneous units with clear-cut borderlines and all members are characterized by a limited number of essential features, while the experiential prototype hypothesis of categorization claims that categories are not homogeneous, but have a prototype, and have very fuzzy boundaries. Category members do not all share the same discrete attributes, but may be linked by family resemblance. It does indeed help to form the cognitive view that categorization is something that underlies the mental processes of language comprehension and language production. And prototype can be defined as some sort of cognitive reference point, "representation of a category" or "ideal" according to the categories to which they are applied, if we take the cognitive view of categories seriously.

When an utterance is being processed, the words call up the corresponding cognitive categories, the mental concepts which we have about the objects in the real world. And also, a cognitive representation of the interaction between the concepts is formed. Thus, the term cognitive context can be reserved for this kind of cognitive representation. The cognitive context is associated in at least two ways with related knowledge stored in long-term memory. On one hand, context-specific knowledge about the categories involved is recalled. On the other hand, other contexts from long-term memory that are somewhat related to it are immediately called up. So in some sense, it can be claimed that we have experienced and stored a large number of interrelated contexts. Cognitive categories are not just dependent on immediate contexts in which they are embedded, but also on the whole bundle of contexts that are associated with them. In other words, the interrelated contexts involved in relevant categories can be organized into a special model that covers all the stored cognitive representations that belong to a certain field. And the way to organize relevant categories is expressed with the term cognitive model. In the following sections, we try to explain the varieties of cognitive models which include frame, schemata, script and plan in terms of language use.

5.2.1 Frame

Frame can be conceived as one way of describing cognitive contexts which provides the background for and is associated with cognitive categories. When Fillmore first used the notion of frame he defined it as:

> any system of linguistic choices — the easiest cases being collections of words, but also including choices of grammatical rules or linguistic categories — that can get associated with prototypical instances of scenes. (qtd. in Ungerer and Schmid 209)

This definition suggests that frame was regarded as an array of linguistic options which were associated with situations. Shifting from the linguistic position, it is more of cognitive interpretation according to the later characterizations of the notion of frame. In 1985 Fillmore said that frames are "specific unified frameworks of knowledge, or coherent schematizations of experience". (223) Later, he also viewed frame as "cognitive structures [...] knowledge of which is presupposed for the concepts encoded by the words". (qtd. in Ungerer and Schmid 209) Self-evidently, the improvement of the definitions and understandings of frame shows that frame has been more and more interpreted in the cognitive sense.

As we have discussed, a frame is a type of cognitive model which represents the knowledge and beliefs about specific and frequently recurring situations. F. Ungerer and H. J. Schmid designed a little story to explain how frame works very well. The story is as follows:

> Sue caught a plane from London to Paris. After she had found her seat she checked whether the life vest was beneath it, but she could not find it. So she asked the flight attendant to find one for her. (Ibid. 211)

The understanding of the story was discussed, focusing on the two occurrences of the definite article "the". According to the rules of English grammar the definite article is used when one assumes that the hearer knows which specific person or thing is being talked about. Given this rule, that "the life vest" and "the flight attendant" in the paragraph are both accompanied by a definite article is difficult to be explained since they are not mentioned at all in the previous text or in the later text. But actually, the two uses of definite article sound so natural and acceptable although they are against the rules of English grammar. This conflict can be explained by "inferences" that are based on our world knowledge. Take the story for example. Everyone who has boarded a plane knows that every carrier provides each passenger with a life vest which is usually stored beneath the seat and that the job of flight attendants is to help passengers. As soon as a plane is mentioned, all of the relevant knowledge about a plane is immediately activated and it is by the knowledge that readers can make the right inferences without effort. Specifically speaking, the cognitive category "plane" would activate a whole bundle of other categories which belong to the "flying on a plane" frame, including pilot, flight attendants, passengers, life vest, safety belt, safety instructions, first class, economy class and so on. Besides the very general frame, there are some subcategories that concern the knowledge of still more specific situations of flight such as eating on a plane, reading magazines, going to the toilet on a plane.

As Minsky suggests, our knowledge should be represented in complex "frame-systems". ① Obviously, within frames cognitive categories acting as anchors and triggers for frames play a major role since frames are designed in the format of categories and their interrelations and frames are also activated by the same categories. Furthermore,

① See Marvin Minsky, "A Framework for Representing Knowledge," *The Psychology of Computer Vision* (New York: McGraw-Hill, 1975) 227ff, qtd. in F. Ungerer and H. J. Schmud, *An Introduction to Cognitive Linguistics* (Beijing: Foreign Language Teaching and Research Press, 2003) 212.

categories can supply their relevant prototypes. These prototypes can successfully lead to some expectations that are based on our own experience and stored in long-term memory. Still take the former story for example. In the subframe of "eating on a plane", we can never expect to have a luxurious meal served on a huge table or with expensive table wares.

Conclusively speaking, frame is a very general cognitive model concerning conceptual-relational knowledge. In the domain of discourse analysis, the application of frame shows three branches, the view of conceptual frame, situational frame and sociocultural frame. (Chen, Zhonghua, and Liu, Xinquan 37—41) The view of conceptual frame is a narrow sense application of frame, holding that frame is only used to show the complex conceptual structures. And the other two views on frame add more senses to the understanding of frame. In the view of situational frame, there is an implicative relationship between frame and situation by which frame is to classify and organize the components in a certain situation. Accordingly, frame must occur with a given situation. Different frame under the background of different situations has different concepts and relations because different situations have different components. In Werth's words, "it is to the situation-type that a frame is related — indeed, perhaps situation-types are rudimentary frames". (111) The view of sociocultural frame brings another property of frame that frames represent various sociocultural differences. In different socioculture, the representation of frame can be different. For example, the frame of restaurant can be different in Africa and in America. The cognitive category of seat may be replaced by cushion in Africa, as Yule states in *Pragmatics*. (87)

As to the cognitive representation of generic intertextuality potentials, the elements in each set of potentials are mainly represented by frame. Specifically, the disciplinary knowledge potentials are represented in the cognitive model of frame with categories of disciplinary theme, disciplinary discourse community, and disciplinary process; the macro-speech act potentials with categories of super-structure, generic structure, and text structure or textual pattern; the evaluation potentials with categories of social subject identity and position of paricipants; modality potentials with categories of other modalities alongside language.

What's more, the subframe within frame such as disciplinary theme and discourse community in the set of disciplinary knowledge potentials may also be represented by the cognitive model of frame. For example, as soon as we refer to the discipline of economy, all of the relevant themes about economy may be immediately activated alongside the discourse communities. It is by the activated knowledge about a certain discipline that we can choose from the disciplinary knowledge potentials to realize generic intertextuality process. Any categories in a frame may activate a whole bundle of other categories.

5.2.2 Schemata

A schema is a structure in semantic memory that specifies the general or expected arrangement of a body of information. Bartlett made an experiment on the guiding function of schemata in the discourse process. He found that when students were given stories that were inconsistent with their schemata, recall was usually distorted in the direction of the schemata. Bartlett suggested that when we encounter an event that differs from our usual understanding, we have difficulty fitting it into our existing schemata and try to avoid remembering it or to alter it until it is consistent with existing schemata.①

Bartlett's famous experiment shows that the appropriate schemata play a very important role in the process of comprehending a story properly. Bartlett's studies suggest that British college students have a very hard time understanding Eskimo folktales and tend to modify many of the details in their recall efforts, producing, in Bartlett's words, "a more coherent, concise, and undecorated tale". (qtd. in Carroll 175) This result successfully proves that comprehension can be very poor when we do not have a schema that corresponds to the story that is unfolding, because it is nearly impossible to see the significance of the events being described. (Carroll 175)

But actually, it is still not enough to have an appropriate schema in memory and we must be able to activate it at the proper time. A series of studies by Dooling and colleagues and by Bransford and Johnson have convincingly demonstrated that comprehension and memory will be poor when the discourse is written so obscurely that we cannot determine what might be the right schema. The passage they took for the experiment is as follows:

> With hocked gems financing him, our hero bravely defied all scornful laughter that tried to prevent his scheme. "Your eyes deceive," he had said, "an egg not a table correctly typifies this unexplored planet." Now three sturdy sisters sought proof, gorging along sometimes through calm vastness, yet more often over turbulent peaks and valleys. Days became weeks as many doubters spread fearful rumors about the edge. At last from nowhere welcome winged creatures appeared signifying momentous success.②

---

① See F. C. Bartlett, *Remembering: A Study in Experimental and Social Psychology* (Cambridge: Cambridge University Press, 1932), for details.

② See D. J. Dooling and R. Lachman, "Effects of Comprehension on Retention of Prose," *Journal of Experimental Psychology* 88 (1971): 216—222, qtd. in David W. Carroll, *Psychology of Language* (Beijing: Foreign Language Teaching and Research Press, 2000) 175—176.

The result of the experiment is that persons who read this passage without the help of a title can remember very little of what was presented, while those who were told the title of the passage was "Christopher Columbus Discovering America" did much better. In other words, once the title of this passage is given and the proper expectation of a proper schema is activated, the passage is to be easily understood.

Up to now, what we have discussed is all the content of a certain schema, or how the expectations of a schema about a certain topic influence the discourse process. By the discussion above, we can conclude some properties of schemata. First of all, schemata are formed in the cognitive process of topic-related information. Or it is the information process that activates schemata. Secondly, when a schema is applied in the construction of global text structure, it represents both the macro structure of text and the structure of expectation. (Chen, Zhonghua, and Liu, Xinquan 43) In this sense, schemata are of perseverance, abstracted from experiences. They are possibly developed with experiences accumulating to be more complex and sophisticated.

According to J. Oller, there are three types of schemata, formal schemata, content schemata and abstract schemata, shown as Fig. 5.1.

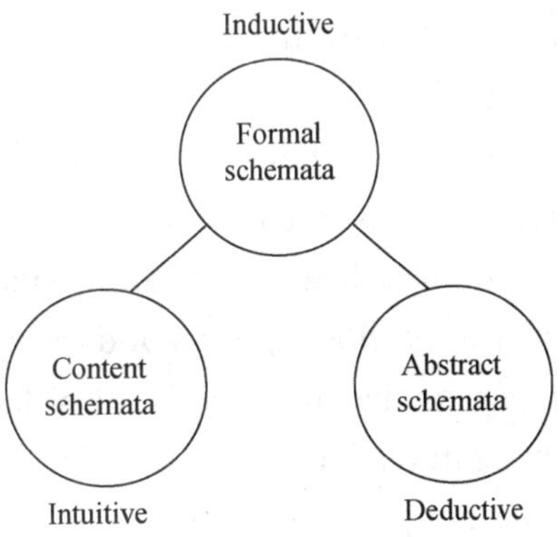

Fig. 5.1 Three types of schemata (Ibid. 45—46)

Content schemata are about specific situation functioning in specific facts or states. But formal schemata are formed by indexical inference, classifying and setting up the inductive relations among the different but comparable categories. For example, a campus is familiar for us, since the space arrangement of buildings is in some sense set or fixed. The space arrangement of buildings in a specific campus is represented in model of content schemata. Different campuses may be designed with different arrangements of buildings, but we can still distinguish campus from factory or park. The schemata we use to recognize are the inductive relations among the cognitive categories. Compared with the former two schemata, what abstract schemata depend on are not the specific facts of states within a given situation, but all relevant ones within all possible situations which are determined by the definition of a semiotic. For example, we define the social functions of university as elites training and academic research. Accordingly, a university must have staff, as well as facilities for research, library and lab. The schema of university comes from the deductive cognition of university by its definition.

Schemata are also used for some components in the sets of generic intertextuality potentials. As we mention in the discussion of super-structure in the set of macro-speech act potentials, besides overall meaning, overall syntax is also needed to define the possible forms in which topics or themes can be ordered in the actual text. In this sense, a schema consists of a series of hierarchically ordered categories, which may be specific for different discourse types and conventionalized and hence different in various societies or cultures.

Schemata provide us with general expectations regarding the way in which information in genres is to be arranged. Take the narrative for instance. Stories typically begin with the introduction of characters and setting. But there are still many different genres for different stories such as detective stories, fairy tales and romances. The typical or expected arrangement of events in a story has been formalized into the concept of a story grammar, featuring a number of typical narrative categories. Generally speaking, story grammars view narratives as consisting of a setting, one or more episodes, and then an ending. In turn, episodes of narrative also have its own structure: some initial event occurs, leading to some internal response on the part of the protagonist.

For the other genres, there are also categories and patterns to arrange the categories. Everyday conversations also have their own schemata. Many conversations, for instance, begin with some kind of greetings exchange, and may be terminated by a sequence of closing turns and leave taking formulas. Scientific discourse, such as journal articles or lectures, may also have a conventional form, which often features an argumentative schema, that is, a number of premises are followed by a conclusion. Similarly, psychological articles may even have a fixed, normative form, which requires an introduction or theory section, an experimental section that has its own subcategories such as design, materials, subjects, and a final discussion section. (qtd. in van Dijk, *News As Discourse* 49) In this way, super-structure is a kind of schemata or represented in the model of schemata. And more specifically speaking, it is a type of formal schemata formed by indexical inference, inducting from the relations among the different but comparable categories.

However, the schemata applied in the cognitive representation of the disciplinary process are abstract rather than formal schemata. Although super-structure is argued to be an evidence to support the underlying abstract logic in disciplinary domains, the underlying abstract logic embedded in the process of discipline is much more than that. The abstract logic represents all the relevant facts and states in all possible situations within a discipline, which is determined by the definition of the disciplinary semiotic system.

5.2.3 Plan

A plan is another model of cognitive representation closely related with schemata.

The most outstanding difference from schemata probably lies in the involvement of human action. It is even regarded as key to settle the dilemmas between stimuli and responses of human activities. (Beaugrande, *Text, Discourse and Process: Toward a Multidisciplinary Science of Texts* 177) Thus, action and interaction emerging from the complex organization of social reality is relevant to plan. Based on these presumptions, Beaugrande illustrates his understanding of plan:

> A plan can be formally represented as composed of pathways leading from one situation or event to another, or on occasion, looping back to a previous one. The plan begins with an initial state and runs to the final state via a progression of intermediate states. A plan is successful if the final state matches the planner's goal state. (Ibid. 178)

Accordingly, the properties of plan are clear. First, plan is closely relevant to goal, or the elements in a plan advance the planner toward a goal, since a plan is successful if the final state matches the planner's goal state. Given a certain goal and the result of the process of decision-making ranging over possible courses of action, the planner may design a plan of action, deciding the steps of plan or in what sequence actions should be performed, continued or terminated. So the second property of plan is that the steps or actions decided by planner must be in a sequence as an operative procedure. In this sense, the component actions of plan must be logically relevant or logically linked and coherent. Considering "a purpose (goal) is a state of mind in which I have a representation of a wanted future state of affairs or event", (van Dijk, *Text and Context: Exploration in the Semantics and Pragmatics of Discourse* 179) "the pathway to a goal or sub-goal is a macro-state in which each action is a micro-state". (Beaugrande, *Text, Discourse and Process: Toward a Multidisciplinary Science of Texts* 179) And in this sense, plans can be described as macro-structures of action, determining which subsequences of actions belong together, how such subsequences are related, and how subsequences may be assigned to one macro-action. The macro-action related to (macro-) purposes determines the actual sequence of actions. (van Dijk, *Text and Context: Exploration in the Semantics and Pragmatics of Discourse* 234)

The model of plan is applied in the cognitive representation of generic structures as well as text structures or textual patterns because generic structures help to realize the stages "which takes us a few steps to reach our goals" and text structures or textual patterns have "a more generalized set of expectations that are shared across a range of texts" about steps to accomplish the goal-oriented action. For example, in the problem-solution pattern, between problem and response there may be an intervening stage in which a plan may occur. (Hoey, *Textual Interaction: An Introduction to Written Discourse Analysis* 140)

It is worthwhile to note that a goal should at least qualify as a desirable state. It seems safe to suggest that desires are both personally and socially defined. Some desirability traits and their negative counterparts are listed by Beaugrande once (Table 5.1).

Table 5.1 A list of desirability traits and their negative counterparts

TYPE OF STATE	DESIRABLE	UNDESIRABLE
PHYSICAL STATE	PH1a health	PH1b illness
	PH2a comfort	PH2b discomfort
	PH3a satisfaction	PH3b need
EMOTIONAL STATE	EM1a happiness	EM1b unhappiness
	EM2a enjoyment	EM2b suffering
	EM3a stimulation	EM3b depression
CHARACTER STATE	CH1a kindness	CH1b unkindness
	CH2a modesty	CH2b vanity
	CH3a honesty	CH3b dishonesty
KNOWLEDGE STATE	KN1a order	KN1b disorder
	KN2a completeness	KN2b incompleteness
	KN3a knownness	KN3b unknownness
	KN4a believability	KN4b unbelievability
	KN5a interest	KN5b boredom
SOCIAL STATE	SO1a attractiveness	SO1b repulsiveness
	SO2a acceptance	SO2b rejection
	SO3a independence	SO3b domination
	SO4a solidarity	SO4b confrontation
ENVIRONMENTAL STATE	EN1a manageability	EN1b unmanageability
	EN2a supportiveness	EN2b contrariness
	EN3a identifiability	EN3b non-identifiability
	EN4a pleasantness	EN4b unpleasantness
STATE TRANSITIONS	TR1a achievement	TR1b failure
	TR2a control	TR2b lack of control
	TR3a directness	TR3b circuitousness
	TR4a economy	TR4b expenditure
	TR5a ease	TR5b difficulty

(Beaugrande, *Text, Discourse and Process: Toward a Multidisciplinary Science of Texts* 180—181)

All of the knowledge about the desirable traits or negative ones are defined by a certain socioculture, which a planner's inferences are based on.

5.2.4 Script

The complexities of desirability can be brought readily under control by scripts. In the model of script, a participant can enter a role, and elements are instructions to participants about what they should say or do in their respective roles. (Ibid. 182) In this sense, script is a kind of plan with social conventions where participants take roles probably in cooperation or interaction with other people.

Since it is a kind of plan, script must bear the properties of plan, goal-oriented and sequential. Take the frame of flying on a plane for example. If we look at it more closely, it turns out that a flight exhibits a very predictable temporal structure in which one stage is often a prerequisite for the next stage. (Ungerer and Schmid 213) Such a sequential perspective can help us refer to the notion of script, the knowledge structures that are particularly designed for frequently recurring event sequences.

In order to make clear the function of script, we would like to introduce another famous example in the literature, the "restaurant" script developed by the computer scientist Roger Schank and the social psychologist Robert Abelson.① Generally the restaurant script can be divided into four scenes including entering, ordering, eating and exiting. Each scene is composed by several actions. Each action is the prerequisite for the next to be performed and the whole scene taken together is necessary for the ensuing scene to take place. Take the entering scene for example. The scene is about the actions that the customer enters the restaurant, looks for a table, decides where to sit, walks to the table and sits down on a chair. Each of these actions is a prerequisite for the next to be performed, and the whole scene taken together is necessary for the ensuing scene to take place in which the meal is ordered. Then how is the ordering scene integrated into the script? Schank and Abelson' figure is shown in Fig. 5.2.

The figure shows that when the scene begins, there are totally three possibilities: there may be a menu on the table, the waiter may bring the menu or the customer may ask the waiter to bring the menu. Once the customer has the menu in hand, the next step is the choice of food. There must be a communication with a waiter who will walk into the kitchen and inform the cook of the order. Again there are two possibilities: the cook may prepare the food or the cook may signal the waiter that no food is available. When it happens, there are again two possibilities: the customer makes another choice of food

① See Roger C. Schank and Roger P. Abelson, *Scripts, Plans, Goals and Understanding* (Hillsdale/N. J., N. Y.: Lawrence Erlbaum, 1977) 42ff, qtd. in F. Ungerer and H. J. Schmud, *An Introduction to Cognitive Linguistics* (Beijing: Foreign Language Teaching and Research Press, 2003) 214—216.

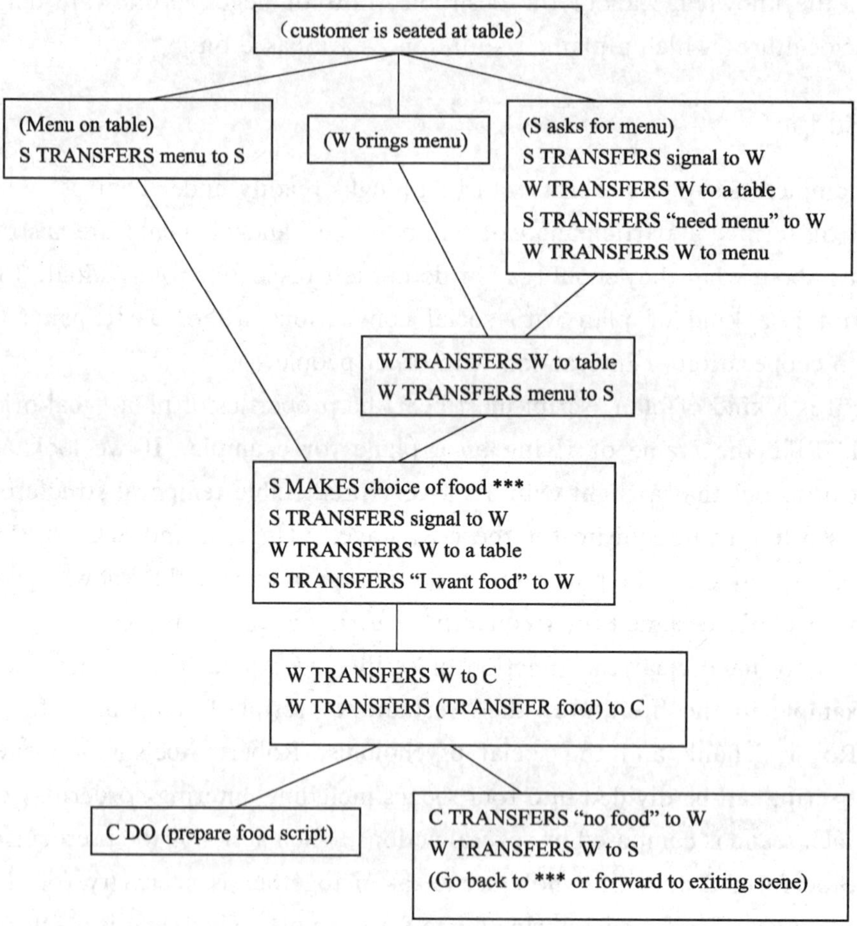

Fig. 5.2 Ordering scene of the "restaurant script" (adapted from Schank and Abelson) (qtd. in Ungerer and Schmid 215)

or decides to leave. The eating and exiting scene can also be represented in the script format in a similar way. The whole business of the restaurant script seems only to translate things that we all know into a format.

The information stored in scripts is so familiar to us that we can hardly realize the fact that we unconsciously fill in an incredible amount of information taken from frames and scripts when we produce or receive information. But if we have a try to understand discourse without supplying the information, we can surely realize the importance and necessity of script. Accordingly, to prove it, two stories in slightly adapted versions from Schank and Abelson were once discussed comparatively.

1) John went into a restaurant. He asked the waitress for coq au vin. He paid the bill and left.

2) John went into a restaurant. He saw a waitress. He got up and went home.

Although the two stories roughly give the same amount of information, the first is perfectly understandable, while the second one does not seem to make sense at all. The reason lies in the fact that the first story fits our script of a meal in a restaurant. We can easily understand that John must have looked at the menu before he ordered and had his meal before paying and finally left. Even the eating scene has never been mentioned in the first story, we still feel it easy to realize it by inference since we have formed a mental representation of the story by our internalized script. In contrast to the first story, the second one fails to correspond to the script expectations. The story only provides a collection of situations that can not be combined into a coherent one. And because of the lack of links between situations, surely we can not follow it easily.

In a conclusion, script is closely related with plan as well as schemata and frame, since script can be realized only if it refers to schema and the logic sequence it must take to reach a goal is consensus with plan. Furthermore, the prototype categories of script represent as frame. "Frames and schemata are more oriented toward the internal arrangement of knowledge, while plans and scripts reflect human needs to get things done in everyday interaction." In other words, "schemas are frame put in serial order, that plans are goal-directed schemas and script socially stabilized plans". (Beaugrande, *Text, Discourse and Process: Toward a Multidisciplinary Science of Texts* 164) So, the distinguishing property of script is that it involves the role of participant representing as one's perspective, habits or conventions in his or her living socioculture, etc. And it may contain personal opinions about the situation as well as opinions which may be instantiations of general, group opinions and attitudes. (Werth 74) It is the role of participant that determines the dynamic and interaction of script.

The social subject identity and position in the evaluation potentials as well as multimodalities in modality potentials are all cognitively represented in the model of script. Social subject identity puts participants into social roles so as to bring the social conventions to them under control by scripts. Position transformation is also guided by scripts which reflect when and where and in what sequence a certain action can occur. For example, with the tendency of marketisation in post-modern society, the positions of roles frequently transform in the script of medical interview, bank consultation and even lecture giving. The selection of modality is also greatly controlled by scripts. For some particular genres, we have formed a script of their multimodalities, which is more or less decided by social conventions or evaluation and attitudes from the groups of society.

5.2.5 Summary

In this section, we argue that the cognitive models as stereotypes of knowledge are used to describe the cognitive representation of generic intertextuality potentials, with the presumption that generic intertextuality potentials are stored as knowledge in long-term memory. The elements of generic intertextuality potentials are cognitively represented by different cognitive models according to their different properties.

Up to now, we only discuss about how the elements of generic intertextuality potentials are cognitively stored and represented, but nothing about how they function in the process of generic intertextuality. In other words, no dynamic mechanism of generic intertextuality process is involved. In order to find the dynamic mechanism, it seems necessary to have a view of integration on the potentials by putting their elements into genres. All genres must bear some of the elements of potentials serving as key criteria to realize generic intertextuality process. How the elements of generic intertextuality potentials in specific genres are referred to realize generic intertextuality process? That is the problem we try to answer in the following section.

5.3 Mental Models of Generic Intertextuality Process

To get the dynamic mechanism of generic intertextualtiy process, we have to take an integrative view of elements of potentials by integrating them into genres. So our perspective of study in the cognitive representation must be transformed into that of genre. As to the cognitive representation of genre, we had better to transform our focus from cognitive models into mental models.

5.3.1 Mental Models and Mental Spaces

Mental model is a conceptual space defined by Johnson-Laird as "human beings understand the world by constructing working models of it in their minds". He even lists what these constructs are responsible for as follow:

> mental models play a central and unifying role in representing objects, states of affairs, sequences of events, the way the world is, and the social and psychological actions of daily life. They enable individuals to make inferences and predictions, to understand phenomena, to decide what action to take and to control its execution, and above all to experience events by proxy; they allow language to be used to create representations comparable to those deriving from direct acquaintance with the world; and they relate words to the world by way of conception and perception. (qtd. in Werth 73)

So, mental models are something that can be used to refer to worlds or serve as spaces to provide the scope for defining worlds. The worlds can be real or imaginary, including elements that do not and cannot have direct reference in the world. (Fauconnier, *Mental Spaces: Aspects of Meaning Construction in Natural Language* XXXVI)

Furthermore, Johnson-Laird also illustrates the primitive elements comprising mental models:

> We [...] organize our experience in terms of temporal and spatial locations, within frameworks of what is possible and permissible, and within a nexus of causes and intentions. The semantic operators provide precisely the framework [...] around which we organize the general knowledge underlying the plausibility of discourse. Semantic fields provide us with our conception of the furniture of the world — of what exists — and the semantic operators provide us with our concept of the various relations that may inhere between these objects. Time and space are primitives that are merely simulated in mental models. Plausibility and permissibility depend on our capacity to construct models of situations that are alternatives to reality and to evaluate them with respect to our knowledge of the 'laws' of nature or morality. (qtd. in Werth 73)

His illustration shows that mental models here are discussed within the domain of discourse representation. They can be constructed in the course of processing a discourse and serve as the configurations of text worlds in which elements probably do not and cannot have direct reference in the real world but the law of nature or morality must be followed. In this sense, text world is the cognitive correlate of the knowledge conveyed and activated by a text use (Beaugrande, *Text, Discourse and Process: Toward a Multidisciplinary Science of Texts* 24) or the cognitive correlate in the mind of a text user for the configuration of concepts activated in regard to a text (Ibid. 77). Hence, it must be in the form of cognitive space or mental space and realized by mental models which are confined to the capacity to construct models of situations that are alternatives to reality and some natural or social conventions.

The notion of mental space is proposed by Fauconnier as an account of cognitive space. It is defined as "domains that we set up as we talk or listen, and that we structure with elements, roles, strategies and relations". Generally speaking, mental spaces are "constructs distinct from linguistic structure but built up in any discourse according to guidelines provided by the linguistic expressions". In short, "mental spaces are represented as structured, incrementable sets — that is, sets with elements and relations holding between them". (Fauconnier, *Mental Spaces: Aspects of Meaning Construction in Natural Language* 16)

What Fauconnier accomplished shows how the full set of recognized problems of reference could be handled with ideas and principles that make sense from a cognitive perspective and mainly applied to the discourse representation, thus developed Discourse Representation Theory. For him, that "mental spaces are represented as structured, incrementable sets" implies "an ordered sequence of ordinary sets, but it will be convenient to speak of the mental space as being built up during ongoing discourse, rather than to refer to the corresponding sequence of sets". (Ibid. 16)

It is the "guidelines provided by the linguistic expressions" that set up mental spaces and are called as "space-builders". (qtd. in Werth 75) In other words, space-builders are contained in linguistic expressions and serve to construct the mental spaces. According to Fauconnier, in the system of mental spaces, a new established space usually originates from the parent space which can be but not always the speaker's reality space. By mapping across different mental spaces, new spaces are established metaphorically connected with their parent spaces.

Although the linguistic form constrains the dynamic construction of the spaces, the construction itself is highly dependent on previous constructions already affected at that point in discourse: available cross-space mappings; available frames and cognitive models; local features of the social framing in which the construction takes place; and, of course, real properties of the surrounding world. (Fauconnier, *Mental Spaces: Aspects of Meaning Construction in Natural Language* XXXIX)

In this sense, space-building is a kind of frame building. The frames provide the abstract-induced schemas that drive mapping across mental spaces. Generally, within cognitive semantics, referential structure is indicated by mental spaces, whereas conceptual structure is indicated by Idealized Cognitive Models and frames, which structure the mental spaces. (Ibid. X—XI) So, in cognitive representation, cognitive models and mental spaces are interdependent and closely related.

5.3.2 Mental Spaces of Genres

It must be pointed out that text world is a mental space but that is not to say mental space can only be of text world. Or not only texts or discourses but also genres can be cognitively constructed into mental spaces. As Beaugrande argues that the spaces in text-world models can be viewed as conceptual macro-states with micro-states inside, (Beaugrande, *Text, Discourse and Process: Toward a Multidisciplinary Science of Texts* 163) we suggest that mental spaces of genres as abstract-induced macro social speech acts can be viewed as the most global abstract conceptual macro-state. The mental space of genre can be used to refer to genre world. The generic components including the elements in generic intertextuality potentials are represented in cognitive models. The reference to the components in cognitive models is to activate their corresponding cognitive models of frames, schemata, scripts or plans, thus driving mapping across mental spaces so as to establish a new mental space for a particular genre.

Mental space configurations of genres are mental models of genres which are to be judged possible or impossible by logic as we judge mental models of reality. The space building is in essence a procedural process in which previously stored knowledge specifies and controls what is done to build a genre world. And the genre world is the cognitive correlate of the knowledge conveyed and activated cognitive models of generic intertextuality potentials which stem from social practices since genre is social event.

According to Fauconnier, the space-building instructions are the same for all uses, the domain types for the mental spaces and the mappings linking the spaces can vary over a wide pragmatic range. (*Mental Spaces: Aspects of Meaning Construction in Natural Language* xlii) Based on the assumption, we argue there is a uniform treatment of multiple genres in terms of mental spaces. But among different genres, domain types for the mental spaces are diverse. Domains are thought to "show up in the form of possible worlds". "The possible worlds contain all referents and their properties. They are fully specified nonlinguistic, and noncognitive." (Ibid. XXXVI)

In the mental spaces of genres, domains should be covered by any possible criteria or generic components which can be used to decide genres. Specifically speaking, the domains can show up in the form of disciplinary world with field or discipline involved, action worlds concerning purposes or goals and corresponding plans to reach goals, evaluation worlds with focus on strategies realized by social identity and position, and modality worlds referring to other modalities that can be applied in particular genres.

The choice of particular spaces or available accessing domains implies different strategies or criteria taken to decide genres. In some sense, the ambiguity of genre definition is yielded by the availability of different types of spaces or different accessing domains.

As we have mentioned, what Fauconnier accomplished was to show how the full set of recognized problems of reference could be handled with ideas and principles that make sense from a cognitive perspective, it is generally realized by mental spaces shown as separate domains of referential structure, connectors between referents within and across spaces, and distinction between roles and individuals and the ability to extend spaces in a discourse. (Ibid. XI) Thus, when we talk about mental space building, we usually refer to the base of the mental space building, the space-builder, and the connector and counterpart to explain shifts taking place.

Genre has been defined in our study as macro social semiosis system which can be abstract-induced as a macro social speech act with micro actions within it. In contrast with discourse representation, genre representation is much of pragmatic, event and function rather than semantics.

Accordingly, we assume that builders of genre mental spaces are not linguistic expressions but categories of components in each domain. Discourse space-builders are understood as linguistic expressions establishing new spaces with elements as well as relations among elements within them; while genre space-builders are categories setting up new spaces with elements as well as underlying logics among elements within them.

For example, in action domain, categories of setting used for events and actions to indicate time, place or other circumstances of a certain episode or even to introduce the characters; complication and resolution defining the episode of the story, and evaluation and a moral, are to establish a genre space of narrative, since they illustrate the plans of actions to reach the goal of the macro speech act narrative as elements as well as underlying logics in the domain. In this way, macro-rules operated in forming categories are strategies for introducing elements into spaces. By macro-rules, we can classify linguistic elements into categories showing the steps of plans in genre representation, thus a genre space in action domain is introduced.

When a genre space is introduced by the space builder of categories, it must be pragmatically connected to its parent space from which the new genre space is mapped. Considering genres as macro social semiosis system enact various types of social contexts, the parent spaces are of the reality of social behaviors in which the triggers are mapped into the targets in the daughter spaces.

As to the referential correspondence, G. Nunberg provides a very important notion of pragmatic function. He shows that we establish links between objects of different nature for psychological, cultural, or locally pragmatic reasons, and the links thus established allow reference to one object in terms of another appropriately linked to it. The general principle is identification principle. (Ibid. 3) It is pragmatic function that serves as connector to link. However, in genre space building, connectors are more of social function, since social events of genres are determined by the conventional rules and social constraints, and enact various types of social contexts. That is to say, the comparison of social function between actions in reality of social behaviors and actions in genre world of communicative behaviors decides the role of connector is to link spaces. For example, in evaluation domain, construction of social identities and positions in reality of social behaviors sets functions or roles in genre world. Thus, identification of social function in reality and in genre world acts as the principle for connection.

5.3.3 Mental Space Integration and Generic Intertextuality

In the different types of domain for genre spaces, different genre spaces are built up. And the different genre spaces are represented in different types of genre spaces determined by domains. The type of space built in the disciplinary domain in which disciplinary knowledge serves as criteria to define genres is disciplinary space. A domain of activity, specifically field of science, can be processed linguistically as a mental space. Disciplinary process abstract-induced in a certain discipline and well accepted by its discourse community is usually illustrated by underlying abstract logic. It is the underlying abstract logic that serves as connectors by the principle of identification to link parent spaces and daughter spaces. The steps or categories generalized within the process are all builders of specific domain spaces. In action domain, there are action spaces in which purposes or goals and corresponding plans to reach goals of actions are all represented. The categories achieved by macro-rules to show the steps of different plans for different goals are builders of action spaces. Evaluation domain corresponds to the evaluation space with social identities and positions as space-builders and system of social evaluation and values as connectors.

However, in modality domain, multimodalities are to be referred to alongside language. In this way, more elaborate space constructions and mappings emerge in the case that they do not seem to include explicit space builders or mapping operators. Multimodality space building involves the blending of sets of spaces. It means that besides the set of spaces built in genre world by language, there are other sets of spaces built in genre world by other signs or other modalities. When multimodalities are simultaneously concerned within a particular genre world, different sets of spaces are blended or integrated. That is actually one perspective of conceptual integration or space blending in genre world. Another perspective of space blending can occur across different types or within a type of spaces. Both of the perspectives of space blending can also be understood as blended space building of generic intertextuality.

5.3.3.1 Space Blending Theory

Space blending is an important cognitive process that drives some of the creativity of thoughts and depends crucially on cognitive mappings between mental spaces. (Fauconnier, *Mappings in Thought and Language* 149) Blending, for Fauconnier, is a simple operation which gives rise to myriad possibilities. In this sense, blending is the central process of conceptual integration constructed cognitively on-line and dynamically. In simple words, blending operates on two input mental spaces to yield a third space, the blend. Two input spaces can be blended if some conditions are satisfied. Some of the conditions are explained as follow:

(1) CROSS-SPACE MAPPING: There is a partial mapping of counter-parts between the input spaces I_1 and I_2.

(2) GENREIC SPACE: There is a generic space, which maps onto each of the inputs. This generic space reflects some common, usually more abstract, structure and organization shared by the inputs and defines the core cross-space mapping between them.

(3) BLEND: The inputs I_1 and I_2 are partially projected onto a fourth space, the blend.

(4) EMERGENT STRUCTURE: The blend has emergent structure not provided by the inputs. This happens in three (interrelated) ways:

COMPOSITION: Taken together, the projections from the inputs make new relations available that did not exist in the separate inputs.

COMPLETION: Knowledge of background frames, cognitive and cultural models, allows the composite structure projected into the blend from the inputs to be viewed as part of a larger self-contained structure in the blend. The pattern in the blend triggered by the inherited structures is "completed" into the larger, emergent structure.

ELABORATION: The structure in the blend can then be elaborated. This is "running the blend." It consists in cognitive work performed within the blend, according to its own emergent logic. (Ibid. 150—151)

It is obvious that cross-space mapping means part of elements in the input spaces are to be mapped. Generic space is a kind of operation space to indicate the shared abstract structures or points by mapping input spaces. Blend implies input spaces being partly projected into the fourth space blended space. And emergent structure is to show the complexity of the blending process. And three principles are used in the process including composition, completion and elaboration. The network of these spaces can be shown in Fig. 5.3.

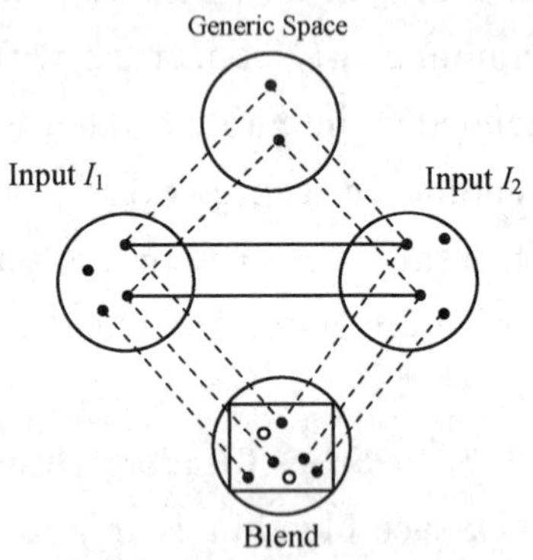

Fig. 5.3 Four spaces in blending theory (Ibid.)

The application of blending theory to genre world actually contains two perspectives, as we have mentioned before, blending by across types or within a type of spaces and by different sets of spaces. Thus, there are totally three dimensions of genre space blending to realize cognitive construction of generic intertextuality space. One is by blending across different types of spaces. Another is blending within a type of spaces. The other one is blending by different sets of spaces. We will discuss in detail about the cognitive process of genre space blending to realize generic intertextuality in the following section.

5.3.3.2 Generic Intertextuality by Space Blending

In genre world, as we argue above, there are four types of spaces corresponding to four domains. Within each of domains, a genre space can be established by different mapping operators and connectors. Thus, different types of spaces are constructed in different domains, varying over a range of cognitive representations of genres. In traditional generic studies, it is reflected as different criteria to define genres.

When we blend different types of spaces into one, the blended space is surely to represent mental space of generic intertextuality. In text linguistic terms, when the elements of other genres are referred to, generic intertextuality occurs. Or the response to the other genres determines the intertextuality of genres. All genres mix together and no hard boarder among them. Hence, genre set, genre network, system of genres or genre colony. Generally speaking, the input spaces of genres can also be mapped by the generic space into the blended space with the emergent structure.

What's more, besides blending across different types of spaces, blending within a type of spaces as well as blending by different sets of spaces can usually simultaneously occur. In other words, a blended space of generic intertextuality is usually an end product of several processes of space blending, or cognitive mappings. The possible multiblending can be shown in Fig. 5.4.

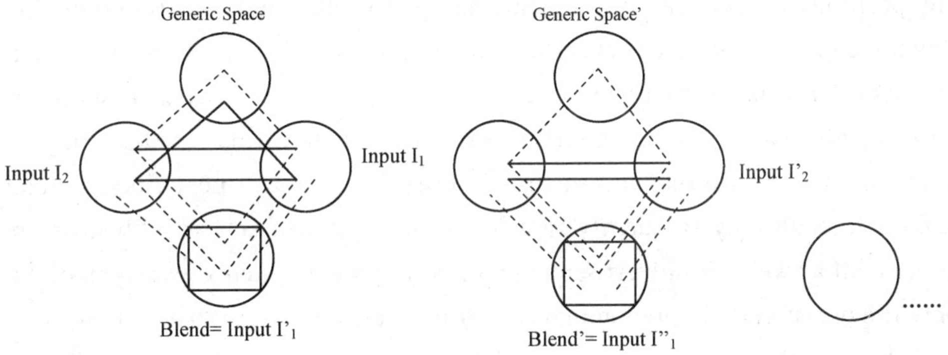

Fig. 5.4 Multiblending of generic intertextuality

Take Rotzoll's analysis of genre advertisement for example. For him, advertisement is a genre which can be recognized as paid, non-personal communication forms used by identified sources through various media with persuasive intent. (94) According to the definition, we can easily locate the different types of spaces in which advertisement genre can be cognitively represented.

First of all, "with persuasive intent" clearly illustrates the goal or purpose of advertisement as persuasion. It functions as space builder to introduce all the actions or steps of plan taken to reach the goal as elements of the space constructed in action domain with connectors of action logic or macro-rules. Specifically speaking, some patterns may be involved to show the actions or steps in plan, such as the desire arousal-fulfilment pattern and problem-solution pattern, to reach the goal of persuasion.

Meanwhile, as paid communication, they are different from common varieties of publicity, or public relations, which are often covered by the media without charge. And by "non-personal" they are distinguished from forms of personal salesmanship occurring in business establishments or door-to-door. Both of them help to construct a space of genre advertisement in evaluation domain. That is to say, in a paid non-personal communication, the social identity of advertiser as well as the social relations or positions of participants in advertisement are set up and act as space builder with connectors of social conventions and systems of values. Evidently, the space built for the paid and non-personal communication is a blended space with the input spaces of paid communication and non-personal communication. The positions of participants vary over a wide range. They may be producers of consumer goods and individuals; producers of consumer goods and retailers and wholesalers; producers of business goods and other business; producers for public relation purposes and individuals, special interest groups and their own employees; producers of consumer and / or business goods and services in international distribution; retailers and individual consumers; individuals and other individuals; and governments, social institutions and special interest groups and the public. (Ibid. 95—96) Any positions of them can be elements in a genre space in evaluation domain.

When elements in different types of spaces such as textual patterns and positions of participants are mapped into a new space, space blending across types of spaces occurs.

Last but not least, advertisement is formed through various media, and are most commonly associated with the mass media of newspapers, magazines, cinema, television, and radio, although they frequently flourish in other forms such as billboards, posters, and direct mail as well. So advertisement can be regarded actually as a symbol package. Not only the use of verbal (predominantly words) but also non-verbal such as music, art, photography, graphics, gestures, etc. can be transformed into pictures in heads. (Ibid. 99)

Obviously, other modalities can be involved in advertisements. Other modality involvement mainly concerns how to say it. The advertiser always faces an almost infinitive number of choices among the verbal and non verbal symbols to implement the advertising strategy. For example, the video disc manufacturer could choose to rely on words and perhaps diagrams to emphasize the end product, i.e. the program on the video disc, with emphasis on arresting scenes from familiar movies. The supplier of drill bits could use action photography of the bit in action supplemented by test data. And the restauranteur could reproduce his entire menu, feature specials, concentrate on atmosphere, the competency of waitresses, or the availability of parking, which all could be implemented through words, pictures, music, sound effects, graphics, and so on. (Ibid. 100) Any modality itself is a symbolic system as language, born with semantic senses. Thus, the involvement of multimodalities itself carries functions, the intentions of various voices for certain purposes or goals. In this way, reference to other modalities can be supporting evidence for generic intertextuality.

Furthermore, there are other convincing studies in mental space construction of other modalities. For example, Karen Van Hoek gives us fascinating evidence for mental space construction in the visual and gesture modality of American sign language. Kress and van Leeuwen's studies on the grammar of visual design provide us very good basis to look into the construction of their mental spaces. Accordingly, space blending may occur among different sets of spaces in different modalities.

Conclusively speaking, by space blending, we can have a blended genre space after the process of generic intertextuality. The elements in the blended space can come from same type of spaces or different types of spaces or different sets of spaces, involving action, evaluation, and multimodalities. Generic space as operation space in space blending indicates the shared abstract structures or points by mapping input spaces. And its emergent structure is to show the complexity of the blending process. In genre space blending, the principle used in the process sensibly depends on fundamental intent carried by genre. For example, the advertiser is identified, which again sets this form of persuasive communication apart from various types of promotion and publicity in the form of news or feature material often carried by the media but supplied by a particular source whose intent is often persuasive. But, finally, advertisements are overwhelmingly used with persuasive intent. That is, the advisers are striving to alter behavior and / or our levels of awareness, knowledge, attitude and so on in a manner that would be beneficial to them. (Rotzoll 94)

So, if our discussion of generic intertextuality process is about how the blending theory is used to reveal the cognitive mechanism of generic intertextuality, the next part of our discussion of generic intertextuality focus is to answer why this part of input spaces is mapped, not the others, or to answer why a subject chooses so with a particular culture and social representation or ideology, or how the spaces blending can happen or what the motivation of the blending is. All of these problems are to be answered by reference to the key notion of intention which controls the focus of generic intertextuality. That is the topic for the next chapter.

Chapter Six

Generic Intertextuality Focus

Genre has been proven to be macro semiosis system in our study. It determines generic intertextuality to be semiotic interaction in semiotic terms. According to Hatim, the two basic levels of semiotic interaction necessarily involve another level of interaction, namely that of speaker or hearer with utterances produced or received. (*Communication across Cultures* 32) It seems that any interaction can not avoid involvement of subjects. Or the success of interaction of utterance with utterance primarily relies on intentionality — the ability to do things with words, the capacity to deploy one's utterance for a purpose. (Ibid.)

Based on the assumption, we propose that the focus of generic intertextuality as interaction is probably one's intention, which controls generic intertextuality process. Because of intentions, users conventionally focus only on specific components from the whole set of resources. Thus, only this but not that part of input spaces is mapped. What's more, in a more global perspective, intentions had to be put under the background of culture and social representation or ideologies. We may well try to explore the role of ideologies functioning on the focus. And by doing so, we try to prove that there is always an interaction between ideology and generic intertextuality. They are mutually influenced and interdependent.

So, in this chapter, we are to discuss what intentions are, in what forms intentions are organized, what role intentions play, how intentions are realized, and even what decides intentions or where intentions come from. By the discussion, we try to answer the questions about why this part of input spaces is mapped, not the others, or to answer why a subject chooses so, or how can the spaces blending happen or what is the motivation of the blending.

6.1 Intentions as Mental Components of Actions

Since only doings with intentions can be taken as actions, (Chen, Zhonghua and Liu, Xinquan 53) intentions must be about actions. Or intention is a necessary component of action. So, if we are to talk about intention, it seems sensible to start from the theory of action which provides a strict and complex system of action.

In the theory of action, some notions involving action are fundamental and widely applied to discourse analysis, mainly doings, acts, actions, events, want, intention as well as purpose and goal. Generally speaking, action is closely connected with event, as shown in the definition of action, "an action is an event brought about by a human being". (van Dijk, *Text and Context: Exploration in the Semantics and Pragmatics of Discourse* 168) In this sense, events are usually treated as units of actions, and actually events are brought about by doings of human beings.

As to event, the most fundamental property is probably change, since the basic concept involved in the definition of the notion of event is change. The change may be viewed as a relation between or an operation on possible worlds or states of affairs. (Ibid.)

According to the definition of event, intention can be regarded as a kind of event because intention can reflect change in one's mind. In this way, intention is event but only mental event. Once intention transforms into goal, it becomes purpose of a certain action. The change from intention into purpose implies a transformation of a mental event into bodily event. If the result of an action is identical with the purpose of the action, the action is called as action of "P-successfulness". If not, it is action of "I-successfulness". For example, if you intent to cash a check in a bank, a mental event happens. If you go to a bank to cash a check, a bodily event occurs. If you successfully cash a check in a bank, you have done an action of P-successfulness. But if you are refused by a bank, there is only an action of I-successfulness. Actions of I-successfulness are referred to by the notion of act. (Chen, Zhonghua and Liu, Xinquan 53—54) And that is why, we define genre as act rather than action in our paper above. Or genres are considered as actions of I-successfulness.

What's more, it is another component of action "want" that controls intention. That is to say, because of a certain want an intention is formed. Usually, wants are consciously recognized, as we often know what we want. So are purposes of our actions. When we take some actions, we normally get ideas of purposes of them. And both of wants and purposes generally refer to consequences or states, specifically ideal consequences or states. From a more global perspective, consequences or states are elements of compound event in the form of process in a sequence of events. In short, they can be taken as points or units of a process.

In contrast with want and purpose, we argue that intention as mental event is more focused on as process rather than point or unit when it plays a role of component in action. Intentions function as link between wants and purposes. It is intention that makes it possible to satisfy want, since a particular action with purpose is derived from intention. As a mental event, intention is actually a sense of what actions being used to satisfy want. It should be located in the control system fed by information about situation, plans, purposes or goals, etc., serving as the central processor of the control system where all cognitive operations take place. (Beaugrande, *Linguistic Theory: The Discourse of Fundamental Works* 290—291)

6.2 Intention as Focus of Generic Intertextuality Process

In the theory of action, it is proposed that there are several types of interactions, including interactions by collective agents, co-agent interactions, and purpose-incompatible interactions. In the first type of interactions, all of agents are to do the same actions with the same intentions and purposes. Collaboration is the necessary condition of this type of interactions. In the second type of interactions, agents cooperate to do compound actions with each agent's actions as components. All of these component actions share the same intentions with the same plans and often the same purposes. Co-ordination is the key to realize purposes. The last type of interaction refers to the interactions with the same intentions and plans but not the same purpose or with totally different intentions or purposes. (Chen, Zhonghua and Liu, Xinquan 54—55)

As to generic intertextuality process, it obviously belongs to the second type of interactions. More than one act of genre are involved in generic intertextuality. Elements of genre spaces in different domains are integrated by co-ordination to realize genre space blending across types of spaces, within a type of spaces, or even across sets of spaces. The key of co-ordination lies in the share of intentions or the maximum of transforming intentions into purposes. Accordingly, the key of interaction among genres or the central processor in control system which corresponds to the generic space in genre space blending should be intention rather than purpose or function or activated knowledge held by cognitive and contextual assumptions.

Generally speaking, integration of genres is under the control of intentions which decide what to choose to blend, why these elements in potentials of generic intertextuality system or those of genre spaces are chosen to be blended and mapped into a new space, and what the motivation of blending is.

6.2.1 Properties of Intentions

The properties of intentions are to be talked about because we believe they may, to some extent, show the mechanism of controlling operation by intentions.

First of all, intentions are mental events. As we mentioned above, it is want that controls intention. Wants provide the actual motivation for our action. If an agent wants the state p to be realized, it is presupposed that he believes that at that moment p is not the case. (van Dijk, *Text and Context: Exploration in the Semantics and Pragmatics of Discourse* 178) But the state, to the agent, is realizable, although it can be only imagined and never to be realized. Because of it, a corresponding intention emerges. In a mental event of intention, want becomes purpose or goal of actions. Since there are always several possibilities to realize want, intention chooses and plans actions that will probably have wanted event or state as a consequence. If the agent expects that his or her chosen and planned actions are to realize the want effectively, the want transforms into the purpose of action.

So, intentions in generic intertextuality process are mental events in which purpose or goals can be defined. According to purpose, agent decides what elements to choose in input spaces and plan structure of moves and blend them into a new space.

Secondly, intention has its macro-structure as proposition or action. It is a pragmatic macro-structure in which a sequence of intentions is subsumed under the more global intentions. The macro-rules used in getting macro-structure of intentions should be the same as those applied in getting that of propositions and actions. The organization of sub-intentions with a more global intention is the same as that of actions with a macro-action. It is represented at various levels, and all of intentions are assigned hierarchical intention structure.

Thus, choice of elements and plan of moves and organization of structure can be controlled by intentions at various levels in a hierarchical intention macro-structure. Applied to generic intertextuality process, the most global intention is to control the most global act which is represented in blended space.

Based on the discussion about properties of intention, we suggest it important to study the most global division of intentions, as well as representation of intentions or in what forms intentions are represented.

6.2.2 Representation of Intentions

When intentions transform into actions, specifically generic intertextuality, purposes or goals are predominant. Both from the perspective of creative writing and literary discourse, and from artificial intelligence by recent work in text pragmatics, there is a similar distinction between managing and monitoring a given situation which is put forward as audience dichotomy akin to the two kinds of audience. The distinction is made mainly depending on purposes or goals of any types of communications. Britton explains the distinction as follows:

> If I describe what has happened to me in order to get my hearer to do something for me, or even to change his opinion about me, then I remain a particular in my own affairs and invite him to become one. If, on the other hand, I merely want to interest him, so that he ... appreciates with me the intricate patterns of events, then not only do I invite him to be a spectator, but I am my self a spectator of my own experience ... As a participant I should be planning ... As a spectator I should be day-dreaming. (qtd. in Hatim, *Communication across Cultures* 33)

It is interesting that in the work in text pragmatics such as in *Introduction to Text Linguistics* by Beaugrande and Dressler, a very similar view in terms of a tendency either to monitor or to manage is also proposed as follows:

> If the dominant function of a text is to provide a reasonably unmediated account of the situation model, SITUATION MONITORING is being performed. If the dominant function is to guide the situation in a manner favorable to the text producer's goals, SITUATION MANAGEMENT is being carried out. (162)

Both of the views take purposes or goals as controlling or predominant focus of speech act by "accommodating communicative use-user distinctions, pragmatic notions such as intentionality, and semiotic categories such as genre and discourse". (Hatim, *Communication across Cultures* 36)

Conclusively speaking, purposes or goals are the other representative forms of intentions from the perspective of action or event and meanwhile involve personal and semiotic sense. That is to say, the global division of purposes or goals may well be taken as representation of the most global intentions as controlling or predominant focus in generic intertextuality process.

For example, with the most global purpose or goal of management aimed at in a particular speech act, both genres of argument and instruction can be referred to. Argumentative and instructional genres, each in its own way, both set out to manage and thus focus on the formation of future behavior, while the means of achieving such an aim are different: the instructional attempt to regulate through instruction without option (as in contrasts, treaties); the argumentative evaluate through persuasion with option (as in advertising, propaganda). (Ibid. 38—39) So, a new problem as how can different means be organized or planned into a whole piece or how intention can be realized arises. We are to talk about it in the next section.

6.2.3 Realization of Intentions

Given a certain want, a corresponding intention forms by decision-making ranging over possible courses of action. The agent may form a particular intention of action which is corresponding with a plan of action to be executed in specific situation fed by various information in different domains. In this sense, we argue that plan is one way to realize intention.

For generic intertextuality dealing with a very complex sequence of actions or interactions, higher organization by a global plan is required. Considering a global plan is "a cognitive macrostructure of intentions, purposes, actions, consequences, goals and strategies", (qtd. in Beaugrande, *Linguistic Theory: The Discourse of Fundamental Works* 294) a plan must be dominated by a macro-action which is the global conceptual structure organizing and monitoring the actual action sequence and defining global goals. (Ibid. 271) Specifically speaking, a plan for generic intertextuality is about how a global purpose or goal is to be reached by a macro-action with a sequence of micro-actions. To reach the goal, elements of micro-actions of genres formed in different domains are chosen to be steps of a plan.

According to van Dijk and Kintsch, plan has both pragmatic and semantic representations. Plan foresees a series of preparatory, component, and terminating speech acts. A macro speech act also has a global propositional content derived from the interaction context and its cognitive counterparts.

Besides plan, strategy is the other way of realizing intention. Actually, plans and strategies together make up the content and style of a global action, with the strategy dominating the moves, that is, the functional actions in a sequence. (Ibid. 271) Evidently, Strategies involve human actions and operate flexibly.

A tactic is an organized system of strategies applying to large segments or periods of lives and actions and influencing the personality of the agent. Tactics are not always good. Bad tactics typically involve conflicting strategies. (Ibid. 272)

According to linguistic and cognitive theories, there are two sets of strategies, local and global strategies. In the generic intertextuality process, both of them are to function and interact in the process, with the global ones determining the meanings of fragments of the whole. Since intentions at different levels in a macro-action of generic intertextuality are organized in a hierarchical structure, strategies as realization of intentions are probably organized hierarchically. Actually, it is strategies that call knowledge stored in cognitive models to provide precisely the relevant information at each point. (Ibid. 272) It is worth noting that knowledge is not provided or expressed, but is accessed and activated to build a kind of background in mental spaces. Thus, strategies serve in overall control system for producing information and representations that are consistent with the overall goals of understanding. (Ibid. 290) In this sense, we may say, strategies themselves are cognitive because what they operate on is relevant to cognitive models and they are operated through their representation of concepts in mind rather than exist in biophysical ways.

It is worthwhile to emphasize that not all of meanings in discourses of generic intertextuality are conscious or intended. In other words, there is usually unconscious or unintended meaning in the text too: a speaker / writer can easily give away his or her hidden motives, can reveal aspects of himself or herself that he or she did not know existed and did not intend to communicate. (Bernard Spolsky 145) This part of meanings is actually determined by ideologies which is to be discussed in the next section.

6.3 Ideology and Generic Intertextuality Process

As we have argued above, we need plans and strategies with functions to rearch purposes or goals of genres. The functions are closely relevant to dominant contextual focus to initially account for the ways generic elements correlates with context. With the dominant contextual focus, the various elements can together establish an orientation towards a particular macro function. The macro function displays the intention which is to determine the macro purpose or predominant purpose, since "texts must ultimately be made to address a single predominant purpose". (Hatim, *Communication across Cultures* 110)

In generic intertextuality process, a number of generic elements are collectively made to function so as to ensure the smooth accomplishment of an overall macro purpose. However, when participating in generic intertextuality or choosing generic elements to function in generic intertextuality process, anyone must be involved in an emotiveness. By this emotiveness, he or she can evaluate how a generic intertextuality can be processed effectively for its ultimate or macro purpose. It may be true that emotiveness is in some sense identical with evaluation which is an all-pervasive phenomenon.

Generally speaking, when we talk about how intentions determine macro purposes or goals, hence overall plans and strategies of generic intertextuality process above, we actually only confine generic intertextuality process to the action domain. If we want to give a relatively comprehensive discussion on generic intertextuality, emotiveness or evaluation must be involved.

Thus, we hold a belief that it is necessary to talk about how there can be emotiveness or evaluation or what influences generic intertextuality participants' emotiveness or evaluation. We are to begin with the notion of ideology as well as the relation between ideology and genres, intending to argue that extra-textual factors such as power and ideology are probably the answer to the problem.

We have mentioned the notion of ideology above when we talk about discourse and its semiotic environments. We proposed that ideology should not be established at the level above that of genre as the fourth plane in the system. Ideologies should be considered as the monitor in the system with many cognitive and social functions at the different levels in the system. The presumption for our proposal is that there are no private or personal ideologies and the belief systems must be socially shared by the members of a social collectivity. And there is inseparable relationship between language and ideology. Or in broader sense, ideology is coextensive with the semiotic field, i.e. with the totality of signifying systems. As Volosinov states in *Marxism and the Philosophy of Language*, the domain ideology coincides with the domain signs. They equate with one another. Wherever a sign is present, ideology is present, too. Everything ideological possesses semiotic value. (qtd. in Xin Bin, *Intertextuality from a Critical Perspective* 34)

So, our study insists on the idea that ideology manipulates generic intertextuality in emotiveness or evaluation domain.

6.3.1 Understandings of Ideology

It has been well accepted that the notion of ideology was first proposed by the French philosopher Destutt de Tracy in 1976 to refer to a "science of ideas". From then on, the notion of ideology has been interpreted in dozens of ways. In *Language as Ideology*, Kress and Hodge define ideology as "a systematic body of ideas [...] a subsuming category which includes sciences and metaphysics, as well as political ideologies of various kinds, without implying anything about their status and reliability as guides to reality." And "language is ideological in another, more political, sense of that word: it involves systematic distortion in the service of class interest". (6) Obviously, ideology in Kress and Hodge's definition is understood in a negative sense. The negative view of ideology is also shared by others such as Marx and Engels, and Althusser, etc. All of them blame ideology on distorting reality. As Althusser defines ideology in his essay *Ideology and Ideological State Apparatuses*:

> It is not their real conditions of existence, their real world, that 'men' 'represent to themselves' in ideology, but above all it is their relation to those conditions of existence which is represented to them there. It is this relation which is at the center of every ideological, i.e. imaginary, representation of the world. It is this relation that contains the 'cause' which has to explain the imaginary distortion of the ideological representation of the real world. (qtd. in Xin Bin, *Intertextuality from a Critical Perspective* 43)

But there are also neutral views of ideology. In a neutral view, ideology is not "a set of ideas which are false, beliefs which betray a distorted consciousness and are therefore politically undesirable". (Ibid. 36) Most typical representatives are probably Fowler, Fairclough, Thompson, Veron and van Dijk. Their neutral views of ideology are generally represented by focusing on two points. One is the focus on the perspective of a particular interest taken to represent the world so as to stress the relatedness of ideology to human interests, as Fairclough stresses. It can be supported by his claim that ideology interpellates subjects, which leads to the view that one of the more significant ideological effects is the constitution of subjects. (Fairclough, *Discourse and Social Change* 87) In other words, it is ideology that realizes the subject constitution and determines the perspective a subject takes to represent the world. The other point is best displayed in Veron's view. For Veron, ideologies are not images or concepts or contents but are sets of rules which determine the organization and functioning of images and concepts. In his own words,

> Ideology is not a particular type of message, or a class of social discourses, but it is one of the many levels of organization of the messages, from the point of view of its semantic properties. Ideology is therefore a level of signification which can be present in any type of message, even in the scientific discourse. Any material of social communication is susceptible to an ideological reading. (qtd. in Xin Bin, *Intertextuality from a Critical Perspective* 53)

Both of the two points represented in the neutral view of ideology are complementary and mutually supported. Perspective taken by subject is a kind of initial stand for subject to organize message; while any set of rules or organization implies a perspective. They are both insightful and provide a sound theoretical basis to argue that ideology may well function as a control focus in emotive or evaluative perspective for any level semiotic process.

6.3.2 Function of Ideology in Generic Intertextuality

Genres have obviously social implications. As Gulich and Raible point out that "linguistic barriers are probably less due to a lack of grammatical competence than to the fact that certain speakers are unable to make use of certain text types, either actively or passively". (qtd. in Hatim and Mason 160—161) The closely relevance between genres and ideology has also been supported by Martin in his report on the results of a large-scale research project. Martin maintains that when ideology is challenged, genres become implicated in a number of ways: which genres a group is able to use and which genres a group chooses to use. That is to say, the choice of genres itself implies ideological sense. As Martin suggests that the use of analytical exposition tends to support the status quo, while hortatory exposition tends to challenge it. (Ibid. 164)

Take a speech by Enoch Powell for example. The speech as follows:

> The first assumption is that the rate of net inflow continues as at present. It has not indeed diminished since the estimate was made, but I am willing to suppose that, especially with the substantially greater limitations which a Conservative government has undertaken to apply, the rate would be markedly reduced during the period in question. For the purposes of argument I will suppose that it fails at a steady rate from 60,000 in 1968 to nil by 1985. in that case the total of the latter year would be reduced by about half-a-million, that is to 3 million.
>
> I now turn to the second and more crucial assumption, the birthrate ... There are grounds for arguing that the immigrant birthrate is likely to rise during the next two or three decades; for instance the proportion of females must increase as dependants join male workers, so that a given total of immigrant population will yield more family units. (Ibid. 161—162)

What Powell seems to be doing is to use analytical exposition for the purposes of presenting immutably some argumentative propositions, although argumentative propositions are usually expected to deliver by argumentation. It seems obvious that Powell deliberately makes his speech look like a detached exposition; while his purpose is still to argue the propositions, which is determined by his intention. Or the deliberate ambivalence in this particular kind of hybridization is clearly ideological.

Conclusively speaking, although intentions determine purposes, hence plans and strategies of genres, they are probably modified to adjust to emotiveness or evaluation which is determined by ideology.

It is also true for generic intertextuality process. Users' intentions bring about macro-purposes which determine plans and strategies of generic intertextuality, specifically, what elements and how to choose from different generic intertextuality potentials in different domains. However, once users' emotiveness or evaluation controlled by ideology is involved, plans and strategies of generic intertextuality are to be modified. That is to say, generic intertextuality focus of intention, in some sense, interacts with ideology. Or it is intentions that determine steps, plans and strategies; while ideology manipulates generic intertextuality process. Both of them play fundamental roles in control system of generic intertextuality.

For example, in *Critical Linguistics: Theory and Application*, Xin Bin analyzes two medical discourses to exhibit how ideology manipulates generic intertextuality process. The two medical discourses are as follow. Silences are marked by sequences of full stops; prolongation of a syllable is marked by colons; interruptions and overlaps are marked by square brackets, and material in round brackets is unclear speech.

Discourse One:

I. D: Hm hm ... Now what do you mean by a sour stomach?

P: ... What's a sour stomach? A heartburn like a heartburn or someth [ing

II. D: [does it burn over there?

P: Yeah

It li- I think I think it like- If you take a needle and stick [Ya right [... there's a pain right here [...

D: [Hm hm [Hm hm [Hm hm

III. D: Hm hm Does it [go into the back?

P: [It is a: ll up here. No. It's all right [up here in the front.

IV. D: [Yeah And when do you get at that?

P: ... wel: l when I eat something wrong.

V. D: How-How soon after you eat it?

P: ... Wel: l ... probably an hour ... maybe [less

D: [About an hour?

P: Maybe less ... I've cheated and I've been drinking which I shouldn't have done.

D: ...

VI. D: [Does drinking make it worse?

P: [(...) Ho ho uh ooh Yes ... ... Especially the carbonation and the alcohol.

VII. D: ... Hm hm ... How much do you drink?

P: ... ... I don't know ... Enough to make me go to sleep at night ... and that's quite a bit.

D: One or two drinks a day?

P: O: h no no no humph it's (more like) ten. [... at night.

D: [How many drinks a night.

P: At night.

D: ...

VIII. ... Whaddya ta- What type of drink? ... I [(...)

P: [Oh vodka

... yeah vodka and ginger ale.

D: ...

IX. ... How long have you been drinking that heavily?

P: ... Since I have been married.

D: ... How long it that?

P: (giggle ...) Four years. (giggle)

Discourse Two:

D: Jody? ... I want to look in your ears. ... Jody?

M: This problem that she has, ... is not ... interfering with her breathing, is it?

C: / Hello / [spoken into ophthalmoscope]

D: No.

M: It just appears that way?

D: Yes. It's very ... it's ... really ... it's like floppy you know and that's why it sounds the way it is.

M: She worries me at night.

D: Yes.

M: Because uh ... when she's asleep I keep checking on her so she doesn't

D: # As you know the important

M: # I keep thinking she's not breathing properly. [spoken while chuckling]

D: as you know, the important thing is that she does have difficulty with the use of her muscles

M: mhm

D: So she has difficulty with the use of her muscles, ... as far as the muscles of her chest, that are used with breathing. Y'know as well as the drooling, the muscles with swallowing, and all that [so all her muscles

M: [Is there some exercise / to strengthen or help that /.

(153—154)

By comparison of the two medical discourses, how ideology influences generic intertextuality is exhibited. The first discourse is a very typical medical discourse in which the doctor controls the interview completely. The plan of the communication is fully determined by purpose representing intention of participants. But in the second discourse, there is obviously generic intertextuality since counseling is involved in the medical discourse. The key to motivate the generic intertextuality is the ideology in current society that is to respect others and to value democracy.

Chapter Seven

Applications in English Teaching

We are deeply convinced that what we have studied in this dissertation about generic intertextuality is both theoretically and practically significant for English teaching, especially in China. But we do not want to claim our methodology or theory is perfect or flawless one. Indeed, we try to emphasize the importance of taking the view of generic intertextuality into account for English teaching in China. A comprehensive survey in generic intertextuality has implications for all domains of English teaching, such as the establishment of English teaching guideline, practical teaching, role of teacher, as well as learning assessment.

For a long time, it has been complained in China that what is being taught in English class is useless and irrelevant to what happens in our later life. English teachers focus more on word pronunciation, vocabulary and sentence grammar. Some ideal sentence patterns or terms are practiced a lot in class. It seems that what we learn in class has nothing to do with social life.

The study on genres has been proven well to make a great contribution to the development of English teaching, especially making up for deficiencies in traditional English teaching. As Zhang Delu states, genre-oriented teaching is to take discourse as the basis of teaching. Teachers transform their teaching focus from vocabulary memory and grammar analysis into discourse interpretation. Discourse is considered as social activity with social communicative functions and interpreted as a whole semantic piece, which is determined by both situational contexts and cultural contexts. (62) Within the framework of genres, what we learn in class is closely relevant to our surroundings in our real life in society.

The rationality of genre-oriented English teaching must be supported by studies on genres. However, as we have mentioned in Chapter Two, in the domain of genre studies, there is always a debate between generic integrity and creation of new genres. In the view of generic integrity, genre is a rhetorically situated and highly institutionalized textual activity, and typical identifiable and ideal discourses of genres are focused. Greatly influenced by the view of generic integrity, our infant stage of genre-oriented English teaching encounters some confusion. For example, genres seem never to be fixed and any efforts to get a fixed division of genres seem to be fruitless. When we link genres with social activities in the real world, it is always true that endless new rhetorical contexts are emerging. Discourses are self-evidently dynamic, constantly developing and often less predictable. Since it is impossible to give definitely fixed genres, the last thing we can do is to choose some identifiable and ideal discourses of genres to analyze. The direct negative effects from this way are obviously to hold down students' creativity and initiative, as well as to leave a gap between discourse and real life.

To settle this confusion, the view of generic intertextuality must be involved, effectively explaining dynamic and mixture of genres. As a matter of fact, the property of intertextuality of genres has been realized and given much attention to. But most of the studies on it are only descriptive not explanatory. The essence or what elements generic intertextuality involves has been seldom discussed. What's more, in the former studies of generic intertextuality, the formal features of generic intertextuality are more concerned. There are almost no conclusive achievements on the cognitive mechanism of generic intertextuality concerning how generic intertextuality happens. All of these deficiencies in studies on generic intertextuality hinder the development of genre-based English teaching. Thus, we believe that our study on generic intertextuality concerning its components and its cognitive mechanism has both theoretical and practical implications for English teaching.

In this chapter, we try to apply what we have achieved to English teaching practice in China, specifically in the respects of establishing teaching guideline, practical teaching, role of teacher, as well as learning assessment.

7.1 Establishment of English Teaching Guideline

In educational enterprise, creativity has long been thought highly of. But English teaching in China seems to routinely discourage creativity by confining students to a limited range of teaching conventions. Teachers provide fixed sets of pre-decided tasks, which results in a loss of motivation among learners since they believe their creativity is not welcomed or restricted. Accordingly, it seems that English teaching in China has nothing to do with creativity with knowledge taught conventionally and routinely.

However, language learning can be of creation and dynamic because genre is assigned a property of innovation and change by generic intertextuality. Members in a certain community are expected to be able to create new forms to respond to new complex rhetorical contexts and convey private intentions within the socially recognized communicative purposes. In this sense, English teaching guideline should be established also with a focus on the cultivation of creativity.

Studies on generic intertextuality provide theoretical basis for the necessity of cultivating creativity in English teaching, and further prove it possible and operable. Our discussion on generic intertextuality system unveils the possible components defining genres that generic intertextuality can refer to. With the help of them, teachers can help students to re-organize incidental facts achieved from discourses of genres cluttered in their minds into a functioning system of potentials. As Beaugrande points out, each batch of poorly digested facts is promptly forgotten after testing, because the systemic organization needed for application is not provided. (*Text*, *Discourse and Process*: *Towards a Multidisciplinary Science of Texts* 278)

It is based on the knowledge of potentials that students can create new forms for any rhetorical contexts and any intentions. As a matter of fact, we hold it as a most effective way to realize cultivation of creativity or make it operable rather than daydream or idle talk. Only when teachers can shift their focus of teaching from memorization of specific facts towards development of a more flexible but powerful strategies to organize and store and apply knowledge, cultivation of creativity can be put into effect. Teachers are consultants and supervisors of class activities who is to encourage students to be themselves and innovative rather tell them messy details or suggest them ways to deal with problems. "Learning materials must not be viewed as incontrovertible artifacts to be swallowed and disgorged under stressful conditions, but only as sample tools for rehearsing the cognitive skills that learners will need for successful thought and action in later life." (Ibid. 279) But meanwhile, teachers may sensibly provide students "resources" to realize innovation and practice initiative. The resources achieved from studies on generic intertextuality system are used to materialize the flexible and powerful strategies which can put cultivation of creativity into effect.

7.2 English Teaching in Practice

As genre is defined as a kind of social event, genre is thought to carry social purpose which is crucial to genre identification and is to be realized by internal structure. It has been supported a lot by Swales, Bhatia, Dudley-Evans, Paré and Smart, Bazerman and Myers in the field of ESP, as well as those in systemic linguistics such as Martin and Rose. Generally speaking, a genre is a staged, goal-oriented social process.

Based on this view, teachers naturally mainly study on formulas and patterns in discourses of genres and apply the achievements into practical teaching. Take teaching of writing for example, students are usually required to follow particular patterns or schematic structures to do their writings, during which their own personality, initiative and creativity are mostly abandoned. As a result, most students well know how to develop a discourse of a certain genre with a certain purpose by a given pattern or structure, but have no ideas about the reasons for the effectiveness of different patterns, the resources they can choose from when dealing with a more complex rhetorical context, the strategies they can apply in developing a discourse with multi-purposes, or the ways in which parts interact. As Richard L. Larson remarks:

> We have, in studies of form, largely a record of search for formulas and patterns in discourse, and a record of advice on the properties that well-ordered discourse ought, in the a priori judgment of theories, to exhibit. But the reasons for the effectiveness of different patterns, the ways in which their parts interact, the most useful techniques of deciding upon particular sequences of steps in composing [...] have been dealt with slightly, hesitantly, or not at all. (qtd. in Beaugrande, *Text, Discourse and Process: Towards a Multidisciplinary Science of Texts* 285)

We believe that what we have done about generic intertextuality can partly solve the problem. Potentials in generic intertextuality system provide resources for students to consider in writing and make it possible for students to fulfill multi-purposes within a discourse. Generic intertextuality process suggests a realistic cognitive activity in responding to any complex rhetorical contexts, which proves the effectiveness of realizing multi-purposes by blending genre spaces in same or different domains. Students are taught not only what can be concerned in writing but also why some of them can be selected to respond to a given context. Both generic intertextuality system and generic intertextuality process involve a comprehensive construction of social meanings, thus guide students to associate writing with social life. In teaching of writing, students are being cultivated to be social individuals. In this way, teaching of writing can never be complained of being far from real life in society.

What's more, what we have argued in generic intertextuality focus can give teachers very good hints of how to encourage students to write and where students should start from in writing. The controlling center of generic intertextuality process is intention in the perspective of action. Students should be encouraged to form motivations, and transform motivations into goals or purposes in writing. By comparing their motivations and current goals in their writing, students are trained to modify or revise their selection of plans and strategies. Any intentions can be realized by so many possible different courses formed by blending various components. Students should be encouraged to be themselves and practice creativity by forming their own courses to realize their intentions. No fixed patterns should be offered for students to copy or imitate.

By the realization of importance of ideology, teachers may well encourage students to reflect on the relation between them as writers and possible readers. According to the focused examination of audience provided in new rhetoric such as Kenneth Burke's theory of identification, as well as the social constructivist approach, second language writing should respond to readers' contexts rather than authors'. In other words, second language writers must take readers' expectations into account in writing. Thus, when Chinese students write in English, they should expect their writings to be read in English contexts. Any courses they select to realize intentions must be acceptable in English communities with their corresponding ideology to manipulate. The important role of ideology in generic intertextuality focus provides a convincing theoretical basis as well as effective operable ways to be in line with readers' expectations. Meanwhile, the attention to the importance of ideology in generic intertextuality suggests the necessity of critical language teaching at various levels and in various domains.

Conclusively, studies on generic intertextuality help students to strike a balance between intention-oriented writing and reader-centered writing.

7.3 Role of Teacher

7.3.1 Interactive Mode in English Class

Since the 1960s, the role of teacher as inspector has changed into consultant or supervisor, which resulted in the transformation of teacher-dominated mode in class into student-centered mode. With the student-centered approach of English teaching as second language, the role of teacher has been discussed a lot. Some believe it is unnecessary to have teachers in English classrooms or at least the importance of teachers has been weakened. Others argue that the important role of teacher can never be denied or teachers play very important roles in facilitating class activities even in student-centered approach.

What we have achieved from our study on generic intertextuality fully supports the important roles of teachers in English teaching as second language. And it further proposes an interactive mode in second language teaching.

Students play active roles in English class. In reading class, for example, students are encouraged to negotiate social meanings with authors. By comprehensive analysis of discourses of genres, students can lead to assumptions about authors' intentions or purposes or goals in discourses so as to get implications in various perspectives. Therefore, students are trained to initiatively participate in reading activities and construct all round social meanings within discourses of genres.

Considering genre spaces can be built in different domains, and the cognitive representation of generic intertextuality is a kind of genre spaces blending, teachers are expected to help students reorganize the accidental facts about generic components in more systematic way and cultivate students' abilities of selecting different components in different domains genre spaces or sets of genre spaces to apply in producing or understanding discourses.

So, on one hand, students should be active and have initiative in learning, since there is always negotiation between producers and receivers. On the other hand, teachers are necessary in delivering knowledge and help students to organize and use perceptual knowledge more systematically and sensibly, as well as to facilitate and activate students' learning. There is actually an interactive mode in English class. The role of teacher evolves and becomes more challenging.

7.3.2 Use of Multimodality in English Teaching

With the development of information or computer technologies, English teaching is assisted with advanced computer equipments and carried out with powerful software. Computer-assistant English teaching or computer-mediated English learning is so popular in China. For example, PowerPoint as a most user-friendly software has been well accepted and widely applied to English teaching. Far distance education by network and multimedia-based teaching are also popular in China's English teaching as second language. In such teaching contexts, some new problems are emerging. One of them is what is the role of teacher in multimedia applied teaching or how we can regard the multimedia applied to English teaching. What we study in generic intertextuality gives some significant revelations of the multimedia.

As we mentioned in the section of modality potentials above, the construction of social semiotics can refer to all kinds of meanings expressed by any social semiotic resources, thus we can use language, in conjunction with other semiotic resource systems and their associated social practices to construct multiple social realities. In this way, there must be an action genre which is realized by other modalities rather than language. In other words, all of modalities may play the same role as language serving as social semiotic resource systems that are formed in society and carry meanings. And any forms of social semiotic resources can realize the three meta-functions as language. Accordingly, genre as macro social semiosis system can be multi-modal, since different semiotic resources or dimensions fulfill different communicative functions. And generic intertextuality can be realized by involvement of multimodalities with modality as component of genre in a broad sense. Or multimodality implies a kind of generic intertextuality.

Considering the multimedia applied to English teaching are actually represented by multimodalities, we hold that the new teaching methods are bringing about new genres by involving generic interextuality in multimodalities. That is to say, we can never take multimedia as tools for teaching but themselves are genres. As House (2005) says that PowerPoint is not only an information medium but also accepted as a genre. (qtd. in Hu, ZhuangLin and Dong Jia 5) So, when teachers give lectures with the assistant of multimedia, they are engaged in a new genre activity. This type of genre activity is of generic intertextuality and represented in various forms such as genre of e-mail, genre of chat room, genre of hypertext, etc.

So, in some sense, the role of teacher in class is the practicer of generic intertextuality by applying multimodalities. And the skills of using multimedia including how to select modalities to construct and deliver meanings in multimedia-based teaching, and how to design the multimodality semiotics can all be instructed by achievements got from studies in multimodality in generic intertextuality. Teachers must realize that material media molded by society for long time can be a semantic resource expressing the meanings for different communities and become modalities, thus modality is socioculture-oriented. By teachers' own performance, students are unconsciously guided to realize the interaction among different social semiosis systems which are surely practical in their later life.

What's more, the involvement of multimodalities brings a new challenge for English teaching. With multimedia, network, and other information technologies introduced in English class, our traditional abilities in reading or writing are not adequate any more. We need "multiliteracy" to respond to the new contexts for language use. Multiliteracy refers to an ability of understanding any information delivered by various modalities and through different media. Hence, as Kramsch (2000) points out, one of the criteria we can use to judge one's mulitliteracy is the degree of his or her familiarity to multimodal technologies. The training of multiliteracy is the urgent task that today's language teachers face up to, since we have entered information technology times in which discourses must be re-defined as generic intertextual processes or products not only involving components in the modality of language but also other multimodalities. And what we have studied on modality potentials in generic intertextuality can be well applied to language teaching with goal of multiliteracy cultivation.

7.4 Learning Assessment

In the English educational enterprise, students' learning must be assessed. It serves as a kind of feedback of students' progress, and gives teachers instruction for further teaching. According to our study on generic intertextuality, there can never be one correct or standard version of understanding of any discourse. Discourses of generic intertextuality can be represented and understood in different dimensions, since they should be viewed as processes rather than products. Producers bear their intentions and transform intentions into purposes or goals and form plans of actions to realize purposes or goals which usually involve different domains with ideology manipulating the steps of whole process. So, we believe what we have studied in generic intertextuality can be well applied to learning assessment, especially in assessment of students' reading comprehension.

Assessment of students' understanding should be a complex concept with many steps as well as various dimensions being involved. Tests by simplified assessment with criteria as correct or not are obviously insufficient and insensible. Any performance of understanding must be concerned within a certain dimension or from a particular perspective. That is to say, understanding, first of all, should be narrowed down to a more specific notion within a definite category. It is probably one of teachers' responsibilities to decide what constitutes understanding. From the macro social semiotic perspective as we have constructed above, semantic construction can be at different levels and in different dimensions. Discourses of genres are always of generic intertextuality, since they are self-evidently complex, dynamic, constantly developing and often less predictable, and most often are seen in hybrid, mixed and embedded forms. And generic intertextuality can be realized by reference to different domains such as disciplinary knowledge, action, evaluation and modality. These domains provide resources for generic intertextuality as well as dimensions for discourse understanding. In different domains, there are different ways and perspectives and strategies to understand. In this sense, understanding is a kind of negotiation between producers and receivers. Manipulated by ideology, they manage to achieve a sensible interpretation of discourse.

Accordingly, we argue a learning assessment should be focused on process of negotiation rather than result of interpretation. Tests must be in form of describing how well students can understand in certain perspectives with relative degrees. Specifically, subjective items or open questions are probably more scientific than objective ones for assessing students' understanding of discourses. Responses for subjective items are more descriptive, illustrating how well students can understand. And the issue of degree must be referred in testing understanding.

What's more, a process of assessing students' understanding itself is a process of understanding. As Bernard Spolsky states, in a test, the question-setter writes to the candidate, who reads this message and writes a response. A third person, the marker, then reads this message and judges it against some more or less implicit criteria. (139) In this sense, there are three active participants in tests of understanding discourses, the producers of discourses, students who try to understand discourses and write responses to them, and teachers as markers who judge students' responses. The relation between teachers and students can thus be considered as that between producers of discourses of responses and interpreters of discourses of responses. As a matter of fact, role of teachers and students can be respectively transformed variously in the whole process of testing. The complication of testing is shown as follows:

Speaker / writer 1	encodes information consciously and unconsciously in
Text 1	the text to be comprehended by
Reader 1	the candidate / test taker who understands it according to previous knowledge, language ability, sense of purpose, etc.; and is then asked by
Speaker / writer 2	who has spoken / written
Text 2	the questions that make up the test to become
Speaker / writer 3	the test-taker answering questions who produces
Text 3	the answers which are read and marked by
Reader 2	the examiner, who becomes in turn
Speaker / writer 4	and produces
Text 4	the grade or score which must be interpreted by
Reader 3	the test-user. (And there may be turtles further down too.) (Ibid. 147)

So, with the transformation of roles, teachers are not only to guide students to understand skillfully but also to apply skills of understanding into practice when they play as readers. To avoid any misunderstanding between teachers and students, negotiation between teachers and students is also needed, in which students have chances to explain why they understand in this way. It further supports the superiority of subjective items and open questions in testing comprehension.

Chapter Eight

Conclusions

8.1 Major Findings and Contributions of the Study

Our study in generic intertextuality is an attempt to build a comprehensive and multi-dimensional framework for generic intertextuality. In our dissertation, we manage to study generic intertextuality in a three-dimensional approach, which correlates with our belief that in language research three dimensions should be taken, pragmatics, cognition and interaction of social contexts. The major findings can be generalized as the following points.

First of all, we take a semiotic perspective view to construct a macro social semiotic rationale for generic intertextuality. The rationale is to make up for the deficiencies or limitations in previous studies in generic intertextuality. Taking partly Saussure's view of language as semiotic, Peirce's approach to semiotic, and Hallidayean view of language as social semiotic, we distinguish genre from discourse and prove genre as macro social semiosis system by our analysis of language as well as its environmental semiotic system, which helps to suggest that generic intertextuality should be considered in essence as relations of components within the semiosis system of genre.

From the macro social semiotic perspective, we can possibly construct a more comprehensive and inclusive theoretical framework for generic intertextuality. Specifically speaking, the view of two dimensions in language study, synchronic and diachronic, in semiology shows the necessity of studying generic intertextuality in a multi-dimensional approach. By partially taking Peirce's approach and putting an emphasis on semiosis as a sign process and the view of interaction and interpretation, we are inspired to refer to the cognitive mechanism and the newly understood sociocultural and the interactive approach. In a word, we combine the inter-organism and the intra-organism or systemic and cognitive and interactive perspective together within the domain of the study of language as social semiotic. Or, we attempt to develop a framework of macro social semiotic by combining the two perspectives.

It is worthwhile to emphasize that within the macro social semiotic framework, discourse is defined as a whole sign which can be located in the corresponding linguistic sign system where it achieves its meaning and value by associative relation and syntagmatic relation; and at the same time as a sign process in which subjects are allocated roles and demarcated where a certain social convention is used or some interaction happens with other signs depending on interpretant. It is on this base that genre can be understood as macro social semiosis system, which helps generic intertextuality study to be conducted in a more global way or at a more macro level. Generic intertextuality can be studied beyond clauses and even discourses. It is a sensible and scientific approach for generic intertextuality study because genre is essentially a social macro speech act.

When we bring the semiotic view into our study in generic intertextuality, we manage to extend our study into a broader sense. Considering a social reality (or a culture) is itself an edifice of meanings — a semiotic construct, and language is one of the semiotic systems that constitute a culture, we go beyond linguistics into social semiotics and take into account as many modalities of communication as we can in our study in generic intertextuality. In this way, we add more into our study of generic intertextuality by broadening previous understandings of genre so as to make our study more comprehensive.

Secondly, in Chapter Four, within the theoretical framework of macro social semiotic rationale, we accomplish a systematic and relatively inclusive account of generic intertextuality resource system in the form of potentials with an intention to answer what are resources for participants to choose in generic intertextuality system. The potentials are generalized according to the achievements from genre studies concerning both interaction and pragmatics, as well as from our analysis on the role of genre in the system of language and its environmental semiotics in a macro social approach. According to the system of language and its environmental semiotics, genre is positioned at the highest plane. Genre itself is a macro semiosis as well as a sign system involving the semiotic process of register. Register can also serve as a semiosis as well as a sign system with components of field, tenor, mode, and their combination which plays an important role in the sign process of discourse. Generally, the system is a network with each of levels or items mutually connected. Register with three variables corresponding with three functions is the central of the network. It decides the system as the functional correlation of different sign systems. In some sense, we do give a more complete and inclusive interpretation of genre in semiotic terms. And our discussion on the potentials is also in a broader sense, taking other possible modalities of communication as one set of potentials.

Thirdly, our study in generic intertextuality explores the cognitive mechanism underlying generic intertextuality process, explaining how the potentials of the system can be chosen from to realize the process of generic intertextuality or the configuration of generic intertextuality system. After discussing the cognitive models used to represent components in the generic intertextuality potentials, we argue the possibility and appropriateness to apply space blending with mental models to explaining the configuration of generic intertextuality or generic intertextuality process. Space blending involves conceptual integration and effectively explains the cognitive mechanism in dynamic and on-line process of generic intertextuality.

Fourthly, we not only talk about how the blending theory can be used to reveal the cognitive mechanism of generic intertextuality but also make an attempt to answer what the motivation of the blending is or what focus of generic intertextuality is. That is to say, we further account for why this part of input spaces is mapped, not the others. By reference to an action theory, we assume that the key notion of intention in the theory of action controls the blending of generic intertextuality. Or according to the theory action, the process of generic intertextuality is ultimately determined by the function of intention.

Fifthly, in a more global perspective, we figure out a system of language and its environmental semiotics which is constructed in a macro social semiotic approach. According to the system, genre is positioned at the highest plane, monitored and in turn influencing ideologies. Ideologies are argued not to be established at the level above that of genre as the fourth plane in the system but considered as the monitor in the system. They have many cognitive and social functions at the different levels in the system. Therefore, we do explore the role of ideologies functioning on the focus of generic intertextuality, thus making clear how to realize the association between generic intertextuality and ideologies, or what is the carrier of ideologies and in what way ideologies function in generic intertextuality. And by doing so, we prove that there is always an interaction between ideologies and generic intertextuality. They are mutually influenced and interdependent.

Conclusively speaking, we attempt to work out a more comprehensive theoretical model for generic intertextuality with three dimensions of generic intertextuality system, generic intertextuality process, and generic intertextuality focus. Our study in generic intertextuality is significant in three respects. First of all, the theoretical model given for generic intertextuality is comprehensive and inclusive since it involves all of three dimensions of language study, pragmatics, social contexts with ideologies and cognition. Secondly, our study is based on a macro social semiotic rationale, which brings semiotic studies into a more global horizon beyond clauses even discourses. It is because of the expanded application of semiotics that generic intertextuality can embrace other modalities of communication in social life. Thirdly, since mental space theory has been proven to be useful to explain various linguistic and non-linguistic phenomena, we make an attempt to apply it to our exploration of the cognitive mechanism underlying generic intertextuality process. In this way, we broaden the horizon for space blending application.

8.2 Limitations of the Study

The aim of our study is to construct a comprehensive and inclusive theoretical model for generic intertextuality in a macro social semiotic approach. Undoubtedly it is a challenging and complex research, and our study can not be perfect. Although we have suggested a three-dimensional framework and made efforts to explore each of them in detail, we have fully realized that what we have done in our study has a lot of limitations.

First of all, our study develops a model for generic intertextuality only theoretically and lacks first hand data analysis. What we have achieved has not been experimentally testified. We can only assume the model for generic intertextuality to be acceptable theoretically, but can not ensure its effectiveness and reliability in practical operation. Even when we apply it to pedagogy, no experiment on its values has been carried out. So, we just show the significance and necessity to pay more attention to the role of generic intertextuality in teaching and illustrate how much English teaching can be influenced by the achievements of our study. But we do not put them into practice to test their feasibility.

Secondly, since our study is based on a macro social semiotic rationale, it is possible and even necessary to refer to other modalities of communication. Although we have taken modality as one set of potentials in generic intertextuality system and mentioned the blending of modalities in generic intertextuality process, the research in other modalities involved in generic intertextuality as well as their concrete representation in the cognitive mechanism underlying generic intertextuality process has not been carried out fully enough in our dissertation.

Thirdly, the third dimension of our model is on generic intertextuality focus, in which the key notion of intention in the theory of action is taken as motivation of genre blending or focus of generic intertextuality. According to our analysis of the system of language and its environmental semiotics in a global way, we realize the important role of ideologies in language studies at any levels. In our study, we do explore the role of ideologies functioning on the focus of generic intertextuality, and prove that there is always an interaction between ideologies and generic intertextuality. They are mutually influenced and interdependent. However, our study more focuses on the influences of ideologies on generic intertextuality. How generic intertextuality influences forming social ideologies is less explored.

Finally, when we apply what we have achieved to pedagogy, we only inquire into some domains of pedagogy, including establishment of teaching guideline, practical teaching, role of teacher and learning assessment. But actually the application of our achievements to pedagogy can involve more domains, such as textbook compilation and teaching assessment. The pedagogical implication in each domain can be explored in more detail. For example, some specific practical teaching, such as teaching of reading, teaching of writing should be treated in detail respectively.

8.3 Further Research

Our study in generic intertextuality is only a tentative research at a very initial stage to draw more attention to generic intertextuality. I hope my crude study can draw forth further studies. There are many researches can be further carried out.

First, each dimension of our model for generic intertextuality provides us a horizon to explore. Take the modality potentials in the dimension of generic intertextuality system for example. Post-modernism which is flourishing in our current society tends to regard every existence as semiotic. It encourages us to reflect on the values of other modalities of communication such as music, pictures, gestures, etc. From the semiotic perspective, all modalities of communication can serve as semiotic systems as language.

Second, further studies in generic intertextuality are suggested to be conducted in particular fields or disciplines. Genre has been proven to be of social identity with particular discourse communities. We boldly assume that generic intertextuality in different discourse communities can have their own characteristics which need to be further explored.

Third, our study is generally about English, but generic intertextuality is not typical in English. It is a popular phenomenon. But considering the long-standing claim that the structure of a language determines the way in which speakers of that language view the world, whether generic intertextuality represents same in different languages is a topic for us to discuss later.

Fourth, Pedagogy is not the only possible field we can apply the idea of generic intertextuality to. Further discussions on how to apply the idea of generic intertextuality to translation and even culture research is significant.

Finally, neither macro study nor micro study can be solitary and completely interdependent. As van Dijk use macro-rules to link macro-structure and micro-structure, we need probe into the key to associate macro studies of generic intertextuality with micro studies. So further research is encouraged on the relationship between linguistic performance or skills and values of generic intertextuality.

In a word, generic intertextuality is a so challenging and valuable topic which offers us a wide horizon to explore further.

Bibliography

[1] Anthonissen C. "Interaction between Visual and Verbal Communication: Changing Patterns in the Printed Media." Critical Discourse Analysis. Ed. Weiss G. and Wodak R. London: Palgrave Macmillan, 2003: 297—311.

[2] Allen, Graham. Intertextuality. London: Routledge, 2000.

[3] Austin, John L. How to Do Things with Words. Oxford: Oxford UP, 1962.

[4] Bakhtin, M. M. "The Problem of Speech Genres." The Discourse Reader. Ed. Adam Jaworskl and Nikolas Coupland. London: Routledge, 1999: 121—132.

[5] Bakhtin, M.M. The Dialogic Imagination. Austin: University of Texas Press, 1983.

[6] Barthes, Roland. S/Z. New York: Hill & Wang, 1974.

[7] Bauman, Richard. A World of Others' Words: Cross-Culture Perspectives on Intertextuality. Oxford: Blackwell Publishing, 2004.

[8] Bazerman, Charles. Shaping Written Knowledge: The Genre and Activity of the Experimental Article in Science. Madison: University of Wisconsin Press, 1988.

[9] Bazerman, Charles. "Systems of Genres and the Enactment of Social Intentions." Genre and the New Rhetoric. Ed. Aviva Freedman and Peter Medway. London: Taylor & Francis, 1994. 79—101.

[10] Beaugrande, Robert de. Text, Discourse and Process: Toward a Multidisciplinary Science of Texts. New Jersey: ABLEX Publishing Corporation, 1980.

[11] Beaugrande, Robert de. New Foundations for a Science of Text and Discourse. New Jersey: Ablex, 1997.

[12] Beaugrande, Robert de. Linguistic Theory: The Discourse of Fundamental Works. Beijing: Foreign Language Teaching and Research Press, 2003.

[13] Beaugrande, Robert de, and Wolfgang U. Dressler. Introduction to Text Linguistics. London: Longman, 1981.

[14] Beebee, Thomas O. The Ideology of Genre. USA: The Pennsylvania State University Press, 1994.

[15] Berkenkotter, C. & Huckin, T. N. Genre Knowledge in Disciplinary Communication: Cognitive/Culture/Power. Hillsdale, N.J.: Lawrence Erlbaum, 1995.

[16] Bhatia, Vijay K. Analyzing Genre: Language Use in Professional Settings. London: Longman, 1993.

[17] Bhatia, Vijay K. Worlds of Written Discourse. New York: Continuum, 2004.

[18] Biber, Douglas. "A Typology of English Text." Linguistics. 27(1989): 3—43.

[19] Bloome, David, and Anne Egan-Robertson. "The Social Construction of Intertextuality in Classroom Reading and Writing Lessons." Uses of Intertextuality in Classroom and Educational Research. Ed. Nora Shuart-Faris and David Bloome. Connecticut: Information Age Publishing, 2004: 17—64.

[20] Bourdieu, Pierre. "Language and Symbolic Power." The Discourse Reader. Ed. Adam Jaworski and Nikolas Coupland. London: Routledge, 1999: 502—513.

[21] Campcell, K. K. and Jamieson, K. H. "Form and genre in rhetorical criticism: an introduction." Form and Genre: Shaping Rhetorical Action. Ed. K. K. Campbell and K. H. Jamieson. Falls Church, Va: the Speech Communication Association, 1978: 9—32.

[22] Carroll, David W. Psychology of Language. 3rd ed. Beijing: Foreign Language Teaching and Research Press; Belmont: Thomason Learning Asia, 2000.

[23] Chandler, Daniel. Semiotics: The Basics. London: Routledge, 2002.

[24] Coe, Richard, Lorelei Lingard and Tatiana Teslenko. "Genre as Action, Strategy, and Difference: An Introduction." The Rhetoric and Ideology of Genre: Strategies for Stability and Change. Ed. Richard Coe, Lorelei Lingard and Tatiana Teslenko. New Jersey: Hampton Press, Inc., 2002: 1—10.

[25] Culler, Jonathan. The Pursuit of Signs: Semiotics, Literature, Deconstruction. London: Routledge, 2001.

[26] Deacon, David, et al. Researching Communications: A Practical Guide to Methods in Media and Cultural Analysis. London: Arnold, 1999.

[27] Devitt, Amy J. "Intertextuality in Tax Accounting: Generic, Referential, and Functional." Textual Dynamics of the Professions. Ed. Charles Bazerman and James Paradis. Madison: University of Wisconsin P, 1991: 336—357.

[28] Dudley-Evans, T. "Genre Analysis and ESP." English Language Research Journal. Ed. Dudley-Evans, T. Vol. 1. Birmingham: the University of Birmingham, 1987: 1—9.

[29] Eggins, S. & Slade, D. Analyzing Casual Conversation. London: Cassell, 1997.

[30] Fairclough, Norman. Discourse and Social Change. Cambridge: Polity Press, 1992.

[31] Eggins, S. & Slade, D. Analyzing Discourse: Textual analysis for social research. London: Routledge, 2003.

[32] Fauconnier, Gilles. Mental Spaces: Aspects of Meaning Construction in Natural Language. Cambridge: Cambridge University Press, 1994.

[33] Fauconnier, Gilles. Mappings in Thought and Language. Cambridge: Cambridge University Press, 1997.

[34] Fawcett, Peter. Translation and Language: Linguistic Theories Explained. Beijing: Foreign Language Teaching and Research Press, 2007.

[35] Fowler, Alastair. Kinds of Literature: An Introduction to the Theory of Genres and

Modes. Oxford：Oxford University Press，1982.

[36] Halliday，M. A. K. Language as Social Semiotic：The Social Interpretation of Language and Meaning. Beijing：Foreign Language Teaching and Research Press；Edward Arnold (Publishers) Limited，2001.

[37] Halliday，M. A. K. An Introduction to Functional Grammar. 2nd ed. Beijing：Foreign Language Teaching and Research Press，2002.

[38] Halliday，M. A. K.，and Christian M. I. M. Matthiessen. Construing Experience Through Meaning：A Language - based Approach to Cognition. London and New York：Continuum，1999.

[39] Halliday，M. A. K. and J. R. Martin. Writing Science：Literacy and Discursive Power. Pittsburgh：University of Pittsburgh Press，1993.

[40] Halliday，M. A. K.，and Ruqaiya Hasan. Language，Context，and Text：Aspects of Language in a Social-Semiotics Perspective. 2nd ed. London：Oxford UP，1989.

[41] Halliday，M. A. K. Cohesion in English. Beijing：Foreign Language Teaching and Research Press，2001.

[42] Hamilton，Heidi E. "Intratextuality，intertextuality，and the construction of identity as patient in Alzheimer's disease." Text. 16.1(1996)：61—90.

[43] Hamilton，Heidi E. Saussure and his Interpreters. Edinburgh：Edinburgh University Press，2003.

[44] Hatim，Basil. Communication Across Cultures：Translation Theory and Contrastive Text Linguistics. Shanghai：Shanghai Foreign Language Education Press，2003.

[45] Hatim，Basil，and Ian Mason. Discourse and the Translator. Shanghai：Shanghai Foreign Language Education Press，2001.

[46] Hoey，Michael. Textual Interaction：An Introduction to Written Discourse Analysis. London：Routledge，2001.

[47] Howarth，David. Discourse：Concepts in the Social Sciences. Buckingham：Open University Press，2000.

[48] Hymes，D. Foundations in Sociolinguistics：An Ethnographic Approach. Philadelphia：University of Pennsylvania Press，1974.

[49] Jaworski，Adam，and Nikolas Coupland. "Introduction：Perspectives on Discourse Analysis." The Discourse Reader. Ed. Adam Jaworski and Nikolas Coupland. London：Routledge，1999：1—44.

[50] Johansen，Jørgen Dines，and Svend Erik Larsen. Signs in Use：An Introduction to Semiotics. Trans. Dinda L. Gorlée and John Irons. London：Routledge，2002.

[51] Johns，Tim. "The Text and its Message." Advances in Written Text Analysis. Ed. Malcolm Coulthard. London：Routledge，1994：102—116.

[52] Johnstone，Barbara. Qualitative methods in Sociolinguistics. Oxford：Oxford University Press，2000.

[53] Kress, Gunther, and Theo van Leeuwen. "Representation and Interaction: Designing the Position of the Viewer." The Discourse Reader. Ed. Adam Jaworski and Nikolas Coupland. London: Routledge, 1999: 377—403.

[54] Kristeva, Julia. Desire in Language: A Semiotic Approach to Literature and Art. New York: Columbia UP, 1980.

[55] Kristeva, Julia. The Kristeva Reader. Oxford: Basil Blackwell 1986.

[56] Lemke, J. L. "Interpersonal meaning in discourse: value orientations." Advances in Systemic Linguistics: Recent Theory and Practice. Ed. Martin Davies and Louise Ravelli. London: Pinter Publishers, 1992: 82—104.

[57] Lemke, J. L. "Ideology, Intertextuality and the Communication of Science."Relations and Functions within and around Language. Ed. Peter H. Fries, Michael Cummings, and William Spruiell. London: continuum, 2002: 32—55.

[58] Lemke, J. L. "Ideology, Intertextuality, and the Notion of Register." Systemic Perspectives on Discourse. Ed. James D. Benson and Williams Greaves. Vol. 1. Norwood, NJ: Ablex, 1985: 175—294.

[59] Lemke, J. L. English Text: System and Structure. Amsterdam: John Benjamins, 1992.

[60] Lemke, J. L. English Text: System and Structure. Beijing: Peking University Press, 2004.

[61] Martin, J. R., and David Rose. Working with Discourse: Meaning beyond the Clause. Beijing: Peking University Press, 2007.

[62] Martin, J. R., and P. R. R. White. The Language of Evaluation: Appraisal in English. New York: Palgrave Macmillan, 2005.

[63] McCathy, Michael and Ronald Carter. Language as Discourse Perspectives for Language Teaching. Beijing: Peking University Press, 2004.

[64] Miall, David S. "Literary Discourse."Handbook of Discourse Processes. Ed. Arthur C. Graesser, Morton Ann Gernsbacher and Susan R. Goldman. Mahwah, NJ: Lawrence Erlbaum Associates, 2003: 321—355.

[65] Miller, C. R. "Genre as social Action." Quarterly Journal of Speech. 70 (1984): 151—176.

[66] Myers, Greg. Writing Biology: Texts in the Social Construction of Scientific Knowledge. Madison: University of Wisconsin Press, 1990.

[67] Morgan, Thaïs. "The Space of Intertextuality." Intertextuality and Contemporary American Fiction. Ed. Partrick O' Donnell and Robert Con Davis. U. S. A: The Johns Hopkins University Press, 1989: 239—279.

[68] Orr, Mary. Intertextuality: Debates and Contexts. UK: Polity Press in association with Blackwell Publishing Ltd., 2003.

[69] Paré, Anthony, and Graham Smart. "Observing genres in action: Towards a research methodology." Genre and the New Rhetoric . Ed. Aviva Freedman and Peter Medway.

London：Taylor and Francis，1994：146—154.

[70] Rotzoll，Kim B. "Advertisements." Discourse and Communication：New Approaches to the Analysis of Mass Media Discourse and Communication. Ed. Teun A. van Dijk. Berlin：Walter de Gruyter & Co.，1985：94—105.

[71] Saussure，F. de. Course in General Lingusitics. Trans. Roy Harris. Beijing：Foreign Language Teaching and Research Press；UK：Gerald Duckworth & Co. Ltd.，2001.

[72] Schiffrin，Deborah. The Handbook of Discourse Analysis. USA：Blackwell Pub，2001.

[73] Spolsky，Bernard. "Comprehension testing，or can understanding be measured?" Language and Understanding. Ed. Gillian Brown，Kristen Malmkjaer，Alastair Pollitt，and John Williams. Oxford University Press，1995：139—152.

[74] Still，Judith and Michael Worton. "Introduction."Intertextuality：Theories and Practices. Ed. Michael Worton and Judith Still. Manchester：Manchester University Press，1990：1—44.

[75] Swales，John M. Research Genres：Explorations and Applications. Cambridge：Cambridge UP，2004.

[76] Thibault，Paul J. "Contextualization and social meaning-making practices." Language and Interaction. Ed. Susan L. Eerdmans，Carlo L. Prevignano and Paul J. Thibault. Amsterdam：J. Benjamins Pub. Co.，2003：41—61.

[77] Thornborrow，Joanna and Shân Wareing. Patterns in Language：Stylistics for Students of Language and Literature. Beijing：Foreign Language Teaching and Research Press，2000.

[78] Todorov，Tzvetan. Genres in Discourse. New York：Cambridge UP，1990.

[79] Ungerer，F.，and H. J. Schmid. An Introduction to Cognitive Linguistics. Beijing：Foreign Language Teaching and Research Press，2003.

[80] Van Dijk，Teun A. Text and Context：Exploration in the Semantics and Pragmatics of Discourse. London：Longman，1977.

[81] Van Dijk，Teun A. News as Discourse. Hillsdale NJ：Lawrence Erlbaum Associates，Inc.，1988.

[82] Van Dijk，Teun A. "The Discourse-Knowledge Interface." Critical Discourse Analysis：Theory and Interdisciplinarity. Ed. Gilbert Weiss and Ruth Wodak. New York：Palgrave Macmillan Ltd.，2003：85—109.

[83] Vološinov，V. N. Marxism and the Philosophy of Language. Trans. Ladislav Matejka and I. R. Titunik. New York：Seminar，1973.

[84] Werth，Paul. Text Worlds：Representing Conceptual Space in Discourse. London：Longman，1999.

[85] Yule，G. Pragmatics. New York：Oxford University Press，1996.

[86] 陈忠华(Chen，Zhonghua)，刘心全(Liu，Xinquan)，杨春苑(Yang，Chunyuan).知识与语篇理解.北京:外语教育与研究出版社，2005.

[87] 胡曙中(Hu，Shuzhong).英语语篇语言学研究.上海:上海外语教育出版社，2005.

[88] 胡壮麟(Hu, Zhuanglin). 社会符号学研究中的多模态化. 语言教学与研究, 1(2007): 1—10.

[89] 胡壮麟(Hu, Zhuanglin), 董佳(Dong, Jia), 意义的多模态构建——对一次 PPT 演示竞赛的语篇分析. 外语电化教学, 3(2006): 3—12.

[90] 胡壮麟(Hu, Zhuanglin), 朱永生(Zhu, Yongsheng). 系统功能语言学概论. 北京: 北京大学出版社, 2005.

[91] 李巧兰(Li, Qiaolan). 皮尔斯与索绪尔符号观比较. 福建师范大学学报, 1(2006): 115—120.

[92] 李战子(Li, Zhanzi). 话语的人际意义研究. 上海: 上海外语教育出版社, 2004.

[93] 钱敏汝(Qian, Minru). 篇章语用学概论. 北京: 外语教育与研究出版社, 2001.

[94] 王铭玉(Wang, Mingyu). 符号语言学. 上海: 上海外语教育出版社, 2006.

[95] 王铭玉(Wang, Mingyu). 从符号学看语言符号学. 解放军外国语学院学报. 27(2004): 1—9.

[96] 辛斌(Xin, Bin). 语篇互文性的批评性分析. 苏州: 苏州大学出版社, 2000.

[97] 辛斌(Xin, Bin). 批评语言学: 理论与应用. 上海: 上海外语教育出版社, 2005.

[98] 熊学亮(Xiong, Xueliang). 认知语用学概论. 上海: 上海外语教育出版社, 2000.

[99] 张德禄(Zhang, Delu). 语类研究的范围及其对外语教学的启示. 外语电化教学. 8(2002): 59—64.